Messages that inspi

'I'm so pleased I discover   ng
time I am feeling truly cr
Love.' – **Alan**

'Thanks so much, you have already helped me out so much just through your blog, book and videos alone!' – **Hazel**

'Inspired by you, I'm going to give up my banking career and be a full time writer and run a foodie/travelogue on YouTube.' – **Bhalasa**

'You really are living the dream. I think I'm in the same situation right now as you were before you decided to quit your job, I'm working the office job in London and going home deflated and exhausted every day! I'll have to make some changes in the near future, hopefully your book will give me some inspiration. Cheers.' – **Conor**

'Hi Mike, firstly thanks for all your work on the blog and book. They're fantastic and partially responsible for my buying a camper last year and planning a route through France and Spain right now. So thanks!

Keep at it mate. You're a painful source of envy for me and a good 8 of my mates. But it's beautiful to see how achievable a genuinely explorative life can be. Thanks.' – **Ben**

'I'm so inspired to do this van and travel Europe even more now I've discovered you and your van' – **Jon**

'Quit my job, sold my house, got divorced (27 yrs). Moved to Oregon, staying with my son. I'm a nurse, minimalist & desire the freedom of Van Life. Read all your info, want to take the plunge.' – **Lucinda**

HOW TO LIVE IN A VAN AND TRAVEL

Mike Hudson

Vandogtraveller.com

ISBN: 978-0-9957050-5-0 (print)
ISBN: 978-0-9957050-4-3 (ebook)
Version one

Edited and proofread by Finn Petcher and Andrew Mowbray

Published 11th June 2017
– Bluedog Books –

Disclaimer: if you wish to apply ideas contained in this book, you are taking full responsibility for your actions.

To those who understood.
And to those who didn't.
Thanks.

Contents

1 - Introduction 9
2 - My story: quit job, build campervan, travel 17
3 - About the van life 27
4 - Get your van 43
5 - Prepare for take off 73
6 - Make a run for it 109
7 - Freecamping & where to stay 127
8 - Toilet & washing 147
9 - Cooking & eating 159
10 - Van safety 173
11 - Travelling happy 187
12 - Entertainment & technology 209
13 - Staying connected 217
14 - Making money on the road 225
15 - Van maintenance & problems 243
16 - Fears, excuses & actually doing it 267
17 - About my van 275
18 - I think that's about it 279

1

Introduction

More and more people are breaking out of their brick homes and moving into vans to live simple, mobile lives led by curiosity, freedom and adventure. A similar thing happened in the 80s (I'll explain that later) but this time it's different. It's not just scruffy people in fields trying to avoid work. This time we have technology and it changes everything.

With just a laptop (powered by solar panels on the van's roof) you can make a living and have a global impact, whether it's from your art, writing, code, photography, music – whatever interests you have. You can even run a business with a team of remote employees working for you. And whilst you're at it, you can be camping in the High Atlas Mountains of Morocco, or exploring the beautiful coastline of the Mediterranean. Or you can spend winter in the Sahara Desert with camels brushing past the van. Goodbye, dull English winter.

You can live anywhere you want. A van is freedom. It's the new office. It's the new home. And no one will be asking for rent.

Thousands of people around the world, young and old, are living the van life right now. Apart from the obvious traveller, adventure seeker and maybe the odd hippy, there's the Google engineer who lives full-time in his truck, and the millionaire baseball player who spends his off-seasons living in his VW camper. We live in vans - our homes and lives are mobile and there has never been a better time to do it.

Three years ago I would sit at my desk every day and think 'this can't be it'. Nothing seemed to make sense. I felt like I was missing out, like there was so much more to life than going back and forth to an office building every day, feeling tired and unfulfilled. I needed to escape. I wanted to explore the world, live in different places, meet different people and let every day be an adventure. I wanted the life I thought might be out there. And if it didn't exist, I'd create it.

The only thing I could think to do was get a van, make it into my full-time travelling home and break away. Off into the sunset. To be free, with the whole of Europe (and possibly beyond) as my garden. But I had no idea how something like this could ever be possible and it stayed as a crazy far-off dream for a while. Apart from having no clue how to make this all happen, I felt like I had to go against everything I'd ever been taught.

I couldn't help but let the obvious questions get in the way: How will I make money? Will I get left behind? Will I end up jobless and broke? How will this look on my CV? Is this safe on my own? Will I ruin my life? And I knew nothing about vans, converting vans or living in vans. All my stuff hardly fits in a house, let alone a van. On top of this I'd only just passed my driving test and the thought of driving a big van on the wrong side of the road, in countries I didn't know, worried me.

But in 2013, I did it. I quit my job, converted a van into my off-grid home and left England to travel Europe and beyond. That was three years ago and I'm still on the road.

My crazy desk-dream has become my reality. Life has gone way beyond my expectations and things I never thought were possible have happened and are happening. This is the best thing I ever did. The life I thought might exist does exist. And although it's just a little bit out of view of what many people call 'normal' life, it is right here and it is an option.

In this book I share with you how I did it – how I used a van to create a mobile life rich in adventure and freedom.

During the time I've been on the road, my blog following has grown to more than 50k followers and four million views. It's been featured all over the world: the front page of Yahoo!, National Geographic, printed publications in the Far East and even on TV across North America. I've had thousands of messages from people all over the world, many supporting me and many of them wanting to do the same thing.

Clearly I'm not the only one with this dream.

On the blog (vandogtraveller.com) you can see the evolution of my whole journey: from where I bought an old rusty van, made it into my home, travelled Europe, to the point where I started to make a living and this whole thing became my normal life.

I've been listening to all the questions I've been getting and making notes for the past two years. Now it's time to put it all into this book. It's the book I wish I had.

Who is this book for?

The overall aim of this book is to help people who are in a similar place to where I was a few years ago: with a dream of travelling in a van, but not knowing where to start or if it's even possible.

This book is for you if:

- You're interested in living and/or travelling in a converted van or vehicle, whether it's short or long term
- You want solutions to the practical problems of living and travelling in a van
- You're wondering if the van life is right for you and you want to get a bit of a taste of what it's like and what's involved
- You have the urge to go out into the world to travel, explore and experience a huge amount of freedom
- You want to know that this can be done – and for as long as you want
- You've always wanted to do this but for whatever reason you STILL haven't

Or maybe you've just finished my first book, *From Van to Home*, and you need a bit of help with the next step: hitting the road. If so, this book is totally for you.

This is more possible than many people think. I will guide

you through everything I've done to make this possible, including my mistakes and lessons. Even if your main fear is about money, I'll show you some of the new options for working that will let you earn money from anywhere – the options we're not taught about.

What I've learnt is that no one will encourage you to have a different or interesting life. Doing a dream is what makes life interesting and exciting, but it can be a lonely pursuit in the beginning. And that's another reason I share what I do. So if you relate to how I felt a few years ago, know that you're not alone.

There are two kinds of messages I often get: the person who says 'I'd love to do this someday' and the person who says 'I wish I did this when I was younger'. There is no difference between these two people – the second person is just older than the first and their dream turned into a regret because they put it on hold. Hoping to do something 'someday' doesn't work. Someday never comes... unless you start today.

And if you are one of those people who message me saying 'I wish I could do that', I want to tell you that you *can* do this. You don't need to know exactly how you'll do everything before you get started. You don't even have to believe that it's possible yet.

What this book isn't

This book doesn't cover the in-depth technical aspects of a van conversion – for example, the electrical system, insulation, plumbing etc. All of that is covered in detail in my other book, *From Van to Home*. I see this book as a continuation from where that book left off. But if you've not yet decided on what van to get, or whether you should buy a camper van or convert a blank van yourself, I've included a whole chapter to give you some guidance. I realise everyone will be at different stages so feel free to skip around as you like.

And if you missed my first book (*From Van to Home*) you can get it here: vandogtraveller.com/van-conversion-book.

Also, this book is based on my experience living in a van and travelling in Europe and North Africa, but most of the information can still be applied to the US and the rest of the world.

One last thing before we start

It's amazing to see that the blog has helped so many people over the past couple of years. I feel so lucky to be able to live the life I do and it's way more rewarding than any salary or an important-sounding job title. If you have spent any of your time to looking at my blog, sharing my posts and joining in on the comments, thank you.

If you have any questions or you want to get in touch you can do it through the blog: vandogtraveller.com.

You'll also find me in these places:

- Facebook page: facebook.com/vandogtraveller
- Instagram: instagram.com/vandogtraveller

I wrote most of this book from my van whilst spending the winter in Morocco. I also wrote some of it in Spain, Hungary, Greece, Italy, Germany and probably others – that's the reason some of the stories might skip around a bit. If you were one of the people who knocked on my van whilst I was 'working on something', this is what I was doing.

Also, any feedback to help me make it better would be really appreciated. If you have any suggestions or recommendations for improvements, or feel there's anything I've missed, just send me a message. It'd be a great help to me and other readers.

Oh yeah, I made an organised list on my blog of some of the products I mention throughout this book. See it here: vandogtraveller.com/van-living-products.

2

My story: quit job, build campervan, travel

1. QUIT JOB

3. TRAVEL

2. BUILD CAMPERVAN

What made me do this in the first place? And what did I do before I lived in a van? I'll briefly explain my story, expanding a bit on the introduction.

A good job

I worked as an electronic systems engineer for a global company in Sheffield, England. I was based in an office but sometimes I'd visit nuclear power plants and other times I'd ride helicopters to work on oil platforms in the North Sea. I was doing alright. I was finally a proper adult with a proper career, contributing to society, and I was able to save some money for the first time in my life. It was exciting for a while.

But, being honest with myself, I wasn't happy. I just felt unfulfilled, uninspired, frustrated and fed up. I thought I'd done everything I'd been taught in order to be happy – get a good education, my own place, a car, a good job and even a girlfriend – yet I'd never felt more unhappy. I was so bored. Life wasn't bad; it was just mundane. And it seemed like everyone around me had accepted this as 'real life'.

I tried to enjoy it. This is how it will be for many years to come and it seemed like everything I'd ever been taught was for this: to get a 'good' job. Or just any job. It would be a lot easier if I could learn to enjoy it (I've learnt to enjoy many things in the past – olives – and I know how amazing the brain is) so that's what I tried to do.

I would repeat on my way to work 'I love my job, I love my life, I love my life'.

I did this for many months. But you can't kid yourself. The things that are missing will still be missing.

The 'real' world

Over winter I'd drive to work in the dark, sit in the office with no windows all day and drive home in the dark. This is what many people do, but thinking about it now, it seems crazy. When I look back at photos of myself from the last year of that job, I don't look healthy. My face is pale and my eyes are like dark grey circles.

I was always tired. I'd come home and couldn't be bothered to do anything. I stopped doing the things I loved, I stopped loving the things I loved, I wasn't exercising, hardly socialising and I had no time or energy to cook good healthy food. But I did have a good job, and I was doing well for myself. I was successful.

I couldn't fool myself that my life was not low quality just because I was earning money. Money does not mean a better quality life. Neither does a granite topped kitchen surface, a new car or a £400 coffee machine.

I know that if I'm bored I'm doing something wrong. I have too many interests to be bored and there's no time to waste. I can't spend the best part of my life wishing my days away. I'd sit at my desk and I'd feel adrenaline bubble up from my stomach. Nothing about it felt right.

What is it for?

I could only ignore the big questions for so long: What am I doing? And why am I doing it? What is a 'good' job anyway? I want a good life not a 'good' job. Are my expectations too high? Maybe I'm spoilt. Maybe I'm an alien.

It bugged me that I didn't seem to know anyone doing what they really wanted in life. It was like everyone was just trying to get on with it.

I was working to run my car to get me to work. I was working to pay rent and bills for a house I spent hardly any time in. I was working to live, pay taxes and maybe secure my freedom in 40 years time. Apart from these things, I didn't really know what I was working towards – or what we, as a society or as a planet were working towards. We exchange our time for numbers on a screen and the numbers on the screen are exchanged for stuff to keep us happy. But for me, it wasn't working. It just seemed like a never ending cycle that makes us tired, fed up and disconnected from our real selves. But it does keep the economy going.

I needed a better reason to be spending 40 to 70 hours per week of my time than to pay taxes and to pay myself. That's a lot of time to spend on something you don't enjoy – it's pretty much your whole life. I felt like I'd fallen into a trap. I was in the wrong place.

The best advice I ever remembered

I wasn't given this advice. I kind of overheard it. I was sat in someone else's class at university. A guy was at the front talking to the whole lecture hall. He said, 'never be in a job you don't like.' He repeated, 'NEVER be in a job you don't like.'

I took the advice.

I quit

I don't want to be one thing for the rest of my life. I don't want to pick something from life's set-menu and be labelled as one single job title forever. I want to be loads of things. I want my life to be full of chapters, not blurred memories of a nine-to-five routine. And I don't want the chapters to be rungs on a career ladder. I want to make my own ladder, putting the rungs in as I go along. And I don't want the ladder to go in a straight line.

In September 2013 I gave my months notice. Even if it was the wrong decision I felt like I had to see for myself, just to make sure. Whatever happened it'd be an adventure.

Too many people around me thought I was reckless for quitting my job. The UK was still coming out of a recession and many people had been let go from their jobs over the past few years. I know I was very lucky to have this job (or any job at all) but I couldn't let that be the reason to carry it on.

My manager asked me all the questions: 'How will you buy clothes and food and fuel?', 'How will you survive?', 'How will you… [fill in the blank]'. I didn't know, and that was my answer. I added something vague like, 'some people are making a living online with just a laptop from anywhere in the world.'. He thought I was mad, and made me think that maybe I was. I didn't know what I was doing. My plan was not a plan, it was just an idea. These conversations repeated for the next few weeks. I couldn't give anyone the answers they wanted.

I could have taken a few months sabbatical or maybe a year out. But I didn't want to come back to work with everything the same. I didn't want a holiday. I wanted to move into something new. To me this was an exit.

I moved out of my house

I told my landlord I'd be gone at the end of the month. I'd furnished the house myself and had one weekend to get rid of everything. I sold some stuff and gave the rest away on the street. I persuaded one guy's wife to let him take the table and chairs off me, insisting there was no catch. I helped him pack it up and forced it all into the boot of his car. Another woman took the bed and the leather sofas. She was running away from her husband and was setting up a secret house to escape. Her husband was yet to know. I thought it was cool we helped each other start new lives.

What am I escaping?

Some people would ask what I was escaping from. They'd talk in this careful tone of voice like they were trying to work out what was wrong with me. No one just quits a good job like that. To these people it was like I'd made the decision to quit actual life. They didn't get it, and I couldn't expect them to.

I was escaping, but not from anything major. It was just from stupid, non-important things that didn't help me in any kind of positive way. But these things seemed to completely surround me. It got me down. I needed to know there was more to life. I was sick of the same stuff. The same smalltalk, the same routine, the news, 'reality' TV, conversations about new kitchens, tiling the bathroom and new cars. I needed to know that life could go deeper than what to me felt like nothing more than meaningless noise and distraction.

But I was mainly on a mission to find new things – new people, places, perspectives. I wanted to create my own path and collect stories, memories and experiences, improvising in my own way as I went along. And what would happen if I kept going down that path? I needed to find out. I didn't care about a salary. I wanted to live by my own definition of meaningful and my own definition of success. And I wanted to learn as much as I could in the process.

Everything pointed to the van thing. It seemed perfect.

From van to home

I bought an old van (an LDV Convoy) and spent the winter fixing it and making it into my full-time home before getting a ferry to France, the European continent and beyond. My aim was to fit it out with everything I needed to live comfortably, off-grid, for a long period of time. It ended up taking five months in total – three months converting the living space and two months making it run properly.

The van was in bad condition. It was rotting and rusted. The engine didn't even start. The voice in my head was constantly saying 'it's not meant to be'. Some days I wouldn't do anything because I was so overwhelmed with what I'd let myself in for. I'd stare at my broken empty van – with the bonnet up and the wheels off and dangling wires that led to nowhere – wondering how it was all going to come together. I took it step by step, learning as I went along and eventually I got there. I'd made my home on wheels. I was ready to live my dream.

I documented the whole conversion process in detail, from start to finish, with notes and annotated photographs. All of that can be found in my other book *From Van to Home.*

I left England

After spending £5500 on the van I had £4500 left to travel with. I set off in March 2014 and I've been living out my desk-dream ever since.

As I write this I'm on the coast of Morocco. I came here for winter. I met a French couple who live in a big truck that's full of musical instruments they picked up in Senegal. Every night we play music and cook on the fire under the stars. I can hear waves crashing right now as I sit in my van writing this. The door is open and the sun is on my face. My brain is happy and it thanks me. There's nothing I feel like I'm missing out on. I'm living and experiencing what feels much more like real life.

Things evolved

My savings lasted me just over one year but I needed to stay on the road. I tried many things and spent a lot of time trying to figure out how I could make this financially sustainable. I was living on pretty much no money at this point: helping out in communities and volunteering in exchange for food.

And then some things happened. Some of my photos went viral. I was getting hundreds of messages and I couldn't keep up. My blog was constantly crashing because of all the traffic. So many different opportunities came up, I didn't know what to do. I was getting offered all sorts of jobs, from motivational speaking to photography to writing – I cannot do any of these things.

People came out of nowhere giving me advice on everything – from how I could make money, how to deal with all the blog traffic, help with hosting and what to do next. I didn't know where these people came from (I never saw them in my old life) but I'm so grateful for their guidance. I felt like a different world was opening up and the people 'in the know' were helping me across to join them.

Now I know who these people are. They are the people living life on their own terms, often travelling the world on a long term basis and creating their own bespoke lifestyles of freedom. And they understand how to use technology to make it all work. My eyes were opened. I started to see what was possible. After 18 months on the road I registered as self-employed and I'm now able to sustain the lifestyle I created.

Life has gone beyond what I thought it could ever be, and all it took was a rusty old van – and to do the opposite of everything I was taught. If I listened to the sceptics, the teachers and, well, most people, I would have missed out on the best and most important chapter of my life so far: the van chapter.

At first, I had no idea how I'd be able to make this all work. But one thing I've learnt is that things evolve in ways that you can never plan for, or even vaguely predict. To not do something just because the end result is not in sight is no good reason not to do it. Things work out. Now I know this for sure.

There have been many moments where I've found it hard to believe the things in front of me. Sometimes I wonder if maybe I've gone crazy. Maybe I slipped away into some fantasy world to try and escape. Maybe I'm still sat at my desk right now. Whatever it is, I'm enjoying it.

I feel successful and fulfilled. I don't care how others define it. My mind has been blown. The world is amazing. Humans are amazing. That's what I needed to know.

3

About the van life

Living in a van is a bit like camping. You can access all sorts of beautiful places whilst living close to nature and having no ties to one fixed location. But it's a lot more comfortable than camping. You have everything with you. You have your books, music, gas and electricity. You can be warm and dry and have proper cooked meals. Everything you need. And you can drive away any time you like. You have the comfort of a house and the benefits of no house. But you do have a home, and the world is your garden.

Everyone who lives in a van does it in their own way. The

versatility and scope for experimentation that a van offers is a big part of why I find this life so interesting and exciting. Through my blog I share with you my way of living the van life and also the lives of others I meet on the road – as well as guided tours of their vans.

But the aim of this book (and the blog) is not to show everyone what a wonderful time I'm having. Nor is it my aim to convince you that you should get a van and live like this. The van life is not for everyone just like the conventional nine-to-five is not for everyone. There are many ways to live. I just want to share what I've found.

In this chapter I'll talk a bit about van life – why some people choose to live in vans, what it means for me and what it can do for you. But first, some history.

The history of van-living

It's only recently that we've started to see a glimpse of van-living in the mainstream – mostly because of the internet. But it has always existed on the fringes. There's a fair bit of history behind van culture and over the years it has run alongside many different subcultures and movements. So here's a van history timeline. By the way, most of this is just my interpretation.

The nomadic life

Until about 10,000 years ago there were hardly any permanent homes or villages. For 95% of our human existence we have lived nomadically, carrying everything we owned around with us – that is, only everything that was absolutely necessary.

So being a nomad isn't such a new thing to us humans. If you see the brain as a result of every iteration that came before it, there's no wonder we have this urge to travel, or that sometimes we feel trapped if we stay in the same place for too long. Why does it feel so good to explore and travel? And why can we sit and stare at a fire for hours in complete contentment? I think it's because it's what we've always done and we recognise it in some subconscious, genetic memory kind of way.

There are still plenty of nomads knocking around. Apart from the modern nomads who use vans and technology (that's us), there are still traditional nomadic tribes who travel by animal, boat or foot and live in tents and temporary shelter.

The vandweller

Vandwelling has its roots as far back as the horse-drawn vehicles such as the Roma Vardo wagons in Europe in the 19th century. I don't know much about this so I've taken this next bit from Wikipedia:

'The first use of the term vandweller was in the United Kingdom Showman and Van Dwellers' Protection Association, a guild for travelling show performers formed in the late 1800s. Shortly afterwards in 1901, Albert Bigalow wrote "The Vandwellers", about people living on the verge of poverty having to live a nomadic life in horse drawn moving vans. After the introduction of motorised vehicles, the modern form of vandwelling began.'

1950s. Introducing, the box on wheels

VW started production of what was basically a 'box on wheels'. It was a huge success and they created many different body variations during the first few years, one of which was the iconic camper that everyone still knows and loves today. VW continued this line of campers up until the 80s. They've gained a cult following and have been the van of choice for generations of hippies, nomads, rockstars, surfers and festival goers.

1960s. The hippies

The 60s came and along with it came good music, LSD and hanging around in fields. People started to break free from social norms, celebrating experimentation and exploring alternative lifestyles. The camper van played an important role – you can't have a cross-country road trip without a psychedelic painted school bus.

1970s. Birth of the free festival

Everything got made illegal and everyone had to get jobs. But some people didn't want the 60s to end so they carried the party on, putting on big free festivals focusing on music, arts and culture. It was all connected by a camping community living in tents and vehicles. Many people decided it would be nice to live like this on a more permanent basis.

1980s. The new-age travellers

Close-knit communities formed, travelling together in their self-built homes made up of wagons, trailers, vans, trucks and buses – anything with wheels. They lived together in semi-permanent locations around the UK, often travelling between music festivals and fairs.

1990s. The rave scene

Several different groups and subcultures merged – including many of the new age travellers and free-festival-people. Sound systems got bigger and psychedelic rock music turned into pounding repetitive beats.

The peak of this period was a huge illegal free festival/rave at Castlemorton Common, England. Over 30 thousand people attended. Convoys of trucks and van-homes gridlocked the surrounding roads. It was all over the national news. New-age travellers and vandwellers have had bad press ever since.

A law was passed as a direct result of this free festival and that's when living in your vehicle became illegal, giving the police the right to detain you if you didn't move on.

This new law made many organisers and sound system owners hit the road, travelling to countries that were less restrictive, using vans and trucks as their homes and to transport the sound systems. This is why England lost a load of young people in the 90s. They're out here in Europe. I've met them. Many never returned to the UK and the parties are still happening.

2000s. The vanlife hashtag

Social media and blogging got big. A guy called Foster Huntington ditched his well paid design job in New York to live out of his camper van and travel the US. He documented it all through his blog and created the 'vanlife' hashtag. This was arguably the start of the whole vanlife movement as most people know it on the internet. It helped introduce this life to many people who never knew it existed.

Mid 2000s. The rise of the digital nomad

With more work being digital based and internet technology getting more advanced, people started to realise that the two hour daily commute to work was a waste of time. They could work from home – or anywhere – as long they had a computer and an internet connection.

And then Tim Ferris released *The 4 Hour Work Week*, a book that introduced this way of working to a far wider audience. More people started to look at work differently, questioning the 'deferred life plan' and many of them radically changing their lives.

Vanlife today

To me, it seems like the van thing is only becoming more and more popular. But my view is biased – I've been immersed in this lifestyle for the past few years. So I looked at some data on Google Trends, which is a tool that graphs the popularity of Google search phrases over time. Searches containing phrases like 'camper van' and 'live in a van' have been steadily increasing for the past decade. The search term 'vanlife' has had an exponentially positive increase since around 2013 – it doubled from 2015 to 2016. It's either that people are using Google more or the van thing *is* growing in popularity.

Why live in a van?

It's different for everyone. A van can be the platform for many different lives. There are all sorts of people living in vans for different reasons. Here are some of them:

Live for less

House living costs take up a considerable amount of most people's monthly earnings. A van bypasses all of that and lets you save the extra money per month which can help you get out of debt, save up, start a business or just buy yourself some time. In this way a van can give you a huge leg up. But it's not just rent. A van can save you a lot of money on hostels and hotels when travelling.

Travel

Travelling in a van is not like normal travelling where you go from point to point, checking in at hostels or hotels on the way, sticking very much to the travel-grid. Having a van gives you access to everywhere and allows you to see places you probably wouldn't see otherwise. You experience all the things in between and get a taste of the whole country. And because you have your home in the back, you can pull up in some amazing spot and live there without being bound by check-in times.

Live your sport

People have always used vans to immerse themselves in their sports – like climbing, skiing or surfing. A van lets you get up when the sun rises to head straight out to do what you love. Your sport becomes your life and a way of living – check out Alex Honnold, a world class solo climber who lives out of his van.

Take a step back

We're constantly being told what to do and how to live, how to look and what to buy. It makes life stressful. Being able to take a step back and distance yourself from all of this can be an invaluable opportunity, and a van lets you do it.

Festivals

Having a van is a nice way to do festivals. It's difficult to go back to a cold, damp tent after having the luxury of a van with full living facilities. Just being able to get up in the morning and make a coffee without getting dressed to queue at a stall makes it worth it. And you can also store loads of food, drink and have your own party at your camp. But when it rains everyone will want come into your van and you'll have to get rid of that wet hippy smell.

Escape winter

I don't know about you but I become like a zombie during the winter, in those three months of darkness. Apart from affecting the regulation of melatonin in the brain, it also makes us deficient in vitamin D, which is not cool. But with a van you can go south for the winter and be a 'snowbird'. This has changed everything for me. I'm so much better and happier when the sky is bright. It's probably why thousands of other people in Europe and the US also do this.

Test out where you want to live

There are so many great cities it's difficult to decide where to live. Living in a van lets you easily try out new places, and even see which neighbourhood you like the best. I always wanted to live in Berlin, so I did, for the whole summer. I tried out all the neighbourhoods and now I know which ones I like the best. That's a city I could live in.

Stay in amazing locations

Living in a van lets you have a view that no one else can even get, and a view that would cost a lot of money if it was a hotel. But this is a view that is all yours. There's nothing better than waking up in a beautiful place and stepping outside to watch the sunrise with a cup of tea.

Health

Many of us are surrounded by distractions, noise, bad food and are often forced to live lifestyles that put a huge amount of stress on our minds and bodies. You might not even realise until you're away from all of these things. But in a van you're forced to be more active and to eat better food – at least that's what I've found. Just by simply living closer to nature, waking up with the sun and going to bed with the sun, we can't help but feel the hugely positive effect it has on us. If that could be put into a pill, Martin Shkreli would buy the patent and make even more billions.

Get back to nature

The sun, the stars, the rhythm of the waves, the sounds of wind and rain and animals. Nature is easy to forget about when living in a house, but in a van you cannot help but be affected by your natural surroundings. And a van is probably the easiest and most comfortable way to live closer to nature.

The ultimate freedom

I will never forget when I was alone with the van for the first time. I was sat in the drivers seat with a full map of Europe in front of me and a full tank of diesel. The physical action of steering the wheel directly affects my life. I can steer myself in or out of any situation or environment I want. I can go anywhere. I am steering my life. Full freedom 24/7.

Live in the now

I used to be constantly thinking about Friday or a holiday or some other event in the future that would take me away from the present. When your mind is not fully in the moment like this you can never be free. Now I'm a lot more present in my everyday life without anything pulling me into the past or the future. I am here in the moment to notice every detail. It's not just the physical freedom of being able to go where you want, but it's also what it does to your head. It sets your mind free.

Live simply and minimally

The best things in life are the simple things. You realise this even more when you live in a van. It lets you see what really matters, and that we don't need all this stuff to be happy or to make our lives complete.

See friends and family

Many of my friends are now spread all over the place. It seems to happen as we get older. But with a van it's much easier to go and visit them for several days or weeks. And because you're totally autonomous, you can just turn up and live outside their house without being a burden on them.

What does vanlife mean for me?

I use my van to move away from the things that don't suit me and towards the things that do. It lets me create a life and path that is truly my own. I can go anywhere I want. If I feel like being alone in the mountains, I can be there by sunset. I can wake up with the sun, the sounds of the forest, the birds, the river or the sea. Outside in nature – this is where our brains evolved to be happy. And if I feel like being in the city, I can go and live there for a while.

For the first time in my adult life I wake up in the morning feeling excited and go to bed feeling excited. I'm not waiting or wishing time away. My days are very different now. The amazing thing is, my quality of life is immeasurably better than my old life, yet it costs a lot less.

Living in a van and travelling has given me good friends and magical experiences. I have memories that will keep me happy and motivated and inspired and hopeful forever. The things that happen and the people I meet often have some kind of significance. I'm able to put my own purpose and meaning to life in a way that wasn't possible before. Also, I don't have that resentment feeling that comes from living my life for someone else, and I no longer feel like I'm caught in someone else's trap.

The other day a photo of the inside of my van got on the front page of Reddit. Some guy was making some 'hipster' comment. If anything starts getting associated with the word 'hipster' it's usually a sign that it's become fashionable in some way. That's fine, but it's not why I'm doing this. I'm not trying to make a statement and I'm not trying to be anything. I don't call myself a 'vanlifer' and I don't call myself a 'digital nomad'. I don't care about these names. I live in a van because it works well for me at this point in my life. I'm doing what excites me and I'm having a nice time. I live in a van for me.

The new American dream

The 'American Dream' was a slogan that came out of a marketing campaign in the 60s, designed to encourage people to borrow money to buy houses they couldn't afford. And then everyone had to borrow more money to fill the house with stuff. Advertising became more effective than ever because now everyone had a TV and a radio in their homes, which made them buy more things and compete with their neighbours.

The debt in the US grew from $160 per person in 1952, to $11,140 per person in 2016 (data from the Federal Reserve). But hardly anyone got any happier.

For this millennial generation, the dream of a perfect house with a driveway and a new car is no longer as desirable as it once was. This is a generation that demands something more meaningful, often without being tied down to one fixed location, and definitely not by debt.

Many people are living in quiet desperation. They're sick and tired and quietly screaming 'I'm tired of this endless cycle of meaningless BS. I want to live and experience life in full and I don't want to wait until I'm 65'. I know this because they tell me. I get their emails.

For many people, having a mobile lifestyle is the new American dream. But this time it's not a marketing campaign. This dream is real, and people are using vans to help them do it.

But it can't all be good, can it?

People often write comments saying things like 'It can't all be good'. They're right. The van life isn't as glamorous as what the #vanlife hashtag on Instagram sometimes makes it out to be. It can be hard work and you have to be prepared to face some challenges. Sometimes you might have to piss in a bottle in the middle of the night. Sometimes you cannot sleep because it's so cold or because you couldn't find anywhere better to camp than the side of a busy motorway. But it's when a few challenges come all at once. That's when it can get difficult.

One time, I was camping alone in the Carpathian Mountains

of Romania. A mouse got in the van. It chewed through every item of food I had and it kept waking me up in the night, scuttling around – it was probably running over my face. I was worried it would get behind the walls and die and rot and smell, or that it would chew through all my careful wiring and woodwork. So I emptied all my stuff onto the road at 2am and stayed up all night trying to catch it.

This was whilst I was ill because a few days before I'd drank some stagnant water from a well. And that's another thing: being ill in a van is uncomfortable and not pretty. I didn't know whether to find a doctor or catch the mouse. But I caught the mouse.

I'd had enough of Romania because it was below freezing and too cold to sleep (I didn't have a heater at this point), so I drove south, all night. I got to Greece. And then the van broke down.

After I fixed the van I locked myself out with the key inside. It was 9pm and dark and I had all my shopping with me. I was trying to get back in without breaking anything. Police came to arrest me and they put me up against the van. They searched me and I thought I was being mugged which made it worse because I was resisting to comply. I didn't believe these fat scruffy guys, dressed in normal clothes, driving an old 4x4, were police. They took everything out my pockets – wallet, phone, money. Thankfully they were police and after they checked me out, they left me to carry on breaking into my own van – I'll explain how to do this later.

So if it helps, that couple of weeks was probably the worst it has got for me. I can laugh at it all now and I feel grateful for these challenges. I love this life. It's all worth it and I feel like the positives easily outweigh any negatives. Or maybe it's that the positives cannot even exist without the negatives. I think so.

And it's not like living in a house

Chances are you've lived in a house most of your life. It's easy to forget how amazing and convenient everything is. All resources are pretty much unlimited and we don't even have to think about it. But that's all about to change. Here are some of the main differences you'll have to adjust to when moving out of your house and into a van (throughout this book I'll explain how to deal with them):

- **Storage and space.** In a house we don't think about how much stuff we have, and space is almost endless. But living in a van forces you to think about and question every possession. Space is very limited – if something comes in, something must go out.
- **Water.** The average person living in a house uses 150 litres of water per day. But in a van you have to make that last two weeks.
- **Toilet.** In a house you flush a lever and let someone else worry about it. In a van we often have to deal with our own waste and dispose of it ourselves.
- **Heating.** Houses are designed to keep you warm in the winter and cool in the summer. We can do our best with insulation and ventilation in a van but it'll never be as good as a house.
- **Washing.** This depends on your van set up but generally you'll have limited facilities and you'll have to find different ways of washing and keeping clean.
- **Noise.** We can do our best to give the van some soundproofing but it'll never be like a double brick wall of a house. If you stay anywhere noisy in your van, and you sleep lightly, you'll probably wake up a few times in the night.
- **Exposure to the elements.** You are much closer to the wind, rain and big thunderstorms. This can be pleasant at times (the sound of light rain) but maybe

not so much at other times (big thunderstorms shaking the van when you need to sleep).

- **You have to find somewhere to camp.** Most of the time this is part of the adventure but sometimes, when you're tired and you've been travelling all day, finding a nice place to sleep is the last thing you want to do.
- **People's attitude.** This will depend on what country you're in but you might have to get used to people's attitudes towards you living in a van – that is, if you care.

These are all challenges that you'll eventually get used to. Humans are good at adapting and we can get used to new things quickly without it affecting our base happiness level. It's only recently we've had warm houses with built in central heating, water and indoor toilets.

Obviously, you need to give yourself time to adjust, and it may take some people more time than others. It took me a good few weeks (maybe months) to properly get comfortable with living in my van, but I knew from the first few nights that this was for me – I found it exciting.

What about money?

People see my photos and assume that this life costs a fortune. One guy commented on one of my Facebook photos saying I 'must have won the lottery or something'. We can't help but associate freedom and good experiences with having loads of money – it's a belief that comes from our social conditioning, the media and pretty much everywhere. But the thing is, I spend way less than I did in my old life, and I probably spend way less per month than the guy making this comment.

It's easy to let money put you off. If you are living in a house, with rent, bills and everything else that comes out of your bank every month, it might seem impossible to live with less money and more freedom. But if you quit all of that and start again with only what you need (like you do when living in a van), you'll see that this life starts to look a lot more possible.

I'll talk a bit about costs and budget in the 'Prepare for take off' chapter. There's also a whole section on making money in the 'Making money on the road' chapter. So I'll save most of the money talk until then. But feel free to skip around.

Warning: vanlife may change you

I got an email from a guy warning me that the longer I live this life of freedom, the harder it will be to go back to 'normal'. I got that email over two years ago. He was right. Once you see what is possible it's difficult to go back.

After 18 months on the road I spent a few weeks in a house. I forgot what it was like and I wanted to remember. It was great – a toilet plumbed into the sewage system and shower with unlimited hot water. But I got fed up after a week. It was lonely. Neighbours didn't speak, I didn't hear the normal outside noises, the sunrise was blocked by buildings and there was always this hum of electricity. I never realised before how much of an effect this has on me.

But back to the warning. After months, or years, on the road, things that you used to enjoy back in your old life might not do it for you anymore. The things you used to think were exciting may no longer be exciting. And worst of all, the people you used to find interesting may not be so interesting anymore. Warning over.

4

Get your van

Getting a van is the first big step. But what van do you get? And do you buy something that is already converted or an empty van to convert yourself? It's important to get a van that's suitable for your needs, so it's worth spending some time thinking about your requirements and looking at a few different vans before you spend all that money. It's easy to get overwhelmed at this point so in this chapter I'll go through some things to think about to help you choose the right van.

Also, buying a second-hand vehicle can be a bit of a gamble

so I'll go through some things to look out for to help you spot any potential problems before you hand over any money.

When I was at this stage I didn't have a clue what to look for. I was spending every spare minute in my break times searching for a van I could make into my home. I didn't know much about vans and I knew nothing about van conversions or the whole camper van world. I'd never even been inside a camper van or motorhome before.

What makes a van liveable?

I'll go through some of the basic amenities that make a van liveable. Near the end of the book, in the 'About my van' chapter, I list all the features of my van, including the specification of the equipment I have onboard. There's also a series of posts I do on my blog called 'van tour' where I show you around other people's vans for inspiration and ideas. See vandogtraveller.com/van-tour.

Kitchen

Most van kitchens are pretty similar, consisting of at least a sink and two gas rings. But you may also have a grill, or an oven in larger conversions. Or some people might just have a portable camping cooker on top of a table. That's fine and they work well but you'll have to spend more money on gas since they usually run on small propane cartridges that tend not to last long for daily use.

You also need some area to prepare food. I have just enough space on the draining board of my sink but if I need more space I can put a large chopping board over the sink and use this as an extra surface.

You may also want to have hot water. In my van I have an instant water heater powered by gas. When I open the hot side of the tap, the boiler automatically ignites and starts heating the water as it comes through. But this isn't essential. You can always just use a kettle on the hob, as many people do.

The kitchen should also include a fridge. They might not be cheap but they are definitely worth it. My fridge runs on 12V so it can be easily powered directly from my van's electrical system. But you can also get fridges that run off either gas, 12V or mains 240V – called '3-way' fridges. Some people have used normal domestic fridges in their vans, but you have to make sure you pick one that has a very high efficiency rating because of the limited power.

Bed and sleeping

If you look at van conversions on the internet you'll come across all sorts of different sleeping arrangements, from bunk beds to hammocks. Whatever you go for, it's important that it's adequate for you to get a good sleep. My advice would be: don't skimp on bed space. Make sure you can fully stretch out in the bed because it makes all the difference.

Also, having a fixed bed that doesn't have to be folded out every night can be useful if there's more than one of you in the van. For example, if one person wants to sleep, the whole bed doesn't have to be pulled out. It's one slightly annoying thing about my van layout – if I'm travelling with friends we might want to sleep at different times, which means most of the living space is taken up by the bed.

Seating

In many van conversions the seating area is used as part of the bed – either for all of the bed or just to extend it. In my van the front of the sofa extends outwards and the cushions all lie flat to make it into the bed.

That's another thing I don't have in my van that would be nice: seats facing each other. When there's more than a few people you have to kind of talk to each other via the wall. Not the most sociable set up but it's alright.

Storage

Typical storage places in a van conversion would be the space under the bed, over the cab and underneath the kitchen unit. But you'll probably also want dedicated storage like drawers, cupboards and shelves. If you don't have enough space for storage inside the van, you can store things on the roof with a roof box or roof rack. I've also seen storage boxes underneath the van (lorries and trucks have these as well) but that's probably something that would have to be custom made for your specific van.

In the next chapter, 'Prepare for take off', I go through where I store the things in my van.

Electricity and power

The electrical system, in the context of a van conversion, is the name given to a battery, wires, fuses and some kind of charging equipment all connected in some way with wires. All this stuff works together to safely provide the electrical appliances in the living space of your van with power. These batteries will be separate from the engine's starter battery and are used for powering everything inside the living area – water pump, lights, fridge and even a computer if you want. In this book I refer to these batteries as 'leisure batteries', but they may also be called auxiliary batteries or living batteries.

The whole electrical system will typically run on 12V (the battery voltage), which means that all your equipment will need to be 12V where possible. One exception is things like chargers (for laptops, cameras, etc.) that need to be plugged into a mains socket. For this you'll need an inverter to convert the 12DC to 240AC.

Note: I wont be going into much more technical detail of a van's electrical system here because it's all covered in depth in my first book, *From Van to Home*, which has circuit diagrams, basic theory, examples and annotated photos of my electrical system.

There are a few ways you can charge your onboard batteries. It's good to have one main method of charging and another as a backup:

- **Solar power.** Solar panels are worth every penny, and they're now cheaper than ever. With a good enough solar setup you won't have to rely on campsites and you can be free to roam anywhere knowing you'll always have power. It's a nice feeling knowing you're getting free power from the sun.
- **Mains hook up.** This lets you plug your van's electrical system into an outdoor mains hookup point, which are often provided by campsites. It will power the inside of the van including a charger for your batteries. In my van I have a mains hook up cable coiled up on the roof in case I ever need it.
- **From the engine.** I have a volt sensing relay (VSR) that I can activate/deactivate with a switch on my control board. A VSR is basically an automatic switch that goes between your engine's alternator and your leisure batteries. When the engine is on, the switch closes and charges your leisure batteries. In the winter, when the solar panels are least effective, I leave the VSR switch on so whenever my engine is running it gives the leisure batteries a bit of a charge.
- **Other.** There are many ways to generate electricity but it's usually down to how practical it would be in a van. I was thinking it could be good to have some kind of dynamo roller thing I could mount my bike to. It would generate electricity to charge my batteries – exercise and power. There are also small

wind generators you can get – I've seen some big truck-homes with these but I'm not sure how well they work.

In my van, the solar panels are the main source of power for charging the leisure batteries. I have 2 x 100W panels fixed to the roof that are constantly charging the batteries (when it's sunny) via a charge controller. This is enough power to run everything. Although, on a couple of occasions I've had to run the engine to stop the batteries from getting too flat. For example, during winter me and a friend were using two computers all day every day for a week and the solar panels couldn't keep up. That's why it can be useful to have at least one other method of charging.

Gas storage

Bottled gas is still the most convenient and cheapest form of portable energy for cooking and heating. You get a huge amount of energy for the space a gas bottle takes up. The cooker in your van will almost always run on gas but you might also have other appliances like a heater that will use the same gas supply.

Most van conversions will either have a refillable gas bottle or an exchangeable bottle that you have to take out and swap with a full one. Pretty much all countries have gas bottle exchange systems where you pay once for the bottle and after this you just pay for the gas when you exchange it. But the problems with this are:

- Gas bottles are not interchangeable between countries
- You have to carry two bottles to be sure you're never without gas – using one bottle while the other is waiting to be exchanged
- The bottles have been in service for many years and you can't always be sure of their safety

- It's expensive – about double the cost of refillable gas

Having a user refillable gas bottle is a much better option for most people in terms of both convenience and cost. You fill it at fuel stations that sell LPG (also called Autogas or GPL, depending on the country), which is basically a non-specific mix of propane/butane (again, this depends on the country), but it's usually mostly propane. And you can top it up any time you like – you don't have to wait until it's empty.

I use an 11kg refillable LPG bottle (made by Gaslow). It can be refilled at fuel stations across the whole of Europe using one of four different adaptors that simply screw onto the filler inlet of the cylinder. I'll talk more later about refilling these gas bottles, as well as what adaptors are needed and where to find filling stations.

Water storage

A built-in internal water tank is probably the most common way to store water in a van conversion. In most cases, a filling point will be mounted externally on the vehicle or in some easy to reach location. But some people may have removable containers that are stored under the sink, in which case you have to lift them in and out of the van to fill them. This is more typical in smaller camper vans.

The size of the tank you choose probably depends on what you'll be using the van for and how long you're going to be away from any source of water. I wouldn't worry about trying to fit in the biggest tank possible out of fear that you may not be able to find water. I've always been able to find water all over Europe and have never had a problem with this.

To give you an idea of consumption, my tank is 70L (I only fill to about 60L) and this lasts me one week, sometimes more, when I'm on my own. I use it mainly for cooking and washing.

About the grey tank

Some van conversions may have a 'grey tank' fitted under the van to collect drain water (grey waste) from the sink and/or shower. A tap is usually fitted to the tank that is opened to dump the grey waste in a more suitable place.

Whether this is needed or not, probably depends on where you are and how you'll be using your van. There are many times when dumping a load of water on to the street – even though it's harmless – looks bad, and for this reason a grey water tank is useful. I wasn't sure if I needed one or not when converting my van, so I installed one just in case. But most of the time I don't use it – I leave the tap open so the grey water goes straight onto the ground like it would without a tank.

Bathroom

A dedicated bathroom is not essential for living in a van and for the amount of room it takes up it might not be so practical, or even possible, in smaller vans. But at the very least you will need some way of going to the toilet in your van – especially in the middle of the night. For this you can use a Porta Potti or just a bucket. I'll explain toilet options later, in the 'toilet & washing' chapter.

In my van I have a bathroom. It's basically a wet room with a shower and a built-in toilet. It is nice to have but It's definitely not a must-have feature (for me, at least). The instant hot water heater I mentioned earlier is also connected to the shower in my bathroom. I'd say this isn't absolutely essential either, and a simple wash down is just as effective, as I'll explain later. Although, the shower head is really useful for washing my hair and also for filling a bucket with hot water to wash clothes in.

Heating your van

I'll mention about van heating in this section because the different options might be useful to know if you're in the stages of choosing your van.

I've only just installed proper heating in my van. It changes everything. Being able to heat the van up before I get out of bed is total luxury – I couldn't even do that in my last house. There are several ways to heat the living space inside your van and they all differ in effectiveness, practicality and safety.

Wood burner

A wood burner will heat the van up very quickly and keep things warm for a long time with little fuel. You can burn all sorts of stuff: peat bricks, logs, twigs, compressed wood shavings. The downside is that you have to actually make the fire, which can be nice and fun to do in the evening, but not so fun when you have to get out of bed on a freezing cold morning and you just want to quickly warm up. Plus you have to actually collect the wood and store it somewhere. Also, it's not so discreet – the smoke coming out the flue makes it obvious someone is living in the van, which might be a problem for some people. But still, there's nothing like a proper open fire.

Also, some burners have a flat top so you can cook food or boil tea on the top. You could also make a DIY heat exchange to give you hot water – copper pipe coiled around the flue. I've not tried it though.

Another thing. If you do have a fire in your van you can get these special 'eco-fans' that help spread the heat around the space, powered by the heat of the fire. It means higher efficiency and less fuel.

The engine

In the winter (and before I got proper heating) I would do most of my driving at night so the residual heat from the cab heater would keep me warm for a few hours. If you're really desperate you could just leave the engine running with the cab heater on, but this isn't so efficient and it's not so good for your engine to do it often. It's also noisy. I've camped next to people who run their engine for heat at night. It's really annoying.

Candles

Even just a couple of candles on their own can give off a surprising amount of heat. Maybe you've seen that video (it went viral a few years ago) of a guy who heats up a room using a candle and two ceramic plant pots – Google 'plant pot heater'. If you're worried about burning normal paraffin candles in such an enclosed space (they are not good to breathe in), you can use soy or beeswax candles.

Gas space heater (or catalytic heater)

These heaters usually use propane gas and some kind of catalyst to produce an efficient and flameless source of heat. They work well for heating things up but they're not the best option for a van. The problem is that they use up oxygen in your living space and they also put a lot of water vapour into the air (a byproduct of burning propane gas) which causes excessive condensation.

Before I installed a proper heater in my van (I'll explain that in a second), this is the type of heater I used. I would turn it on for half an hour at a time which was enough to get things very warm. It did the job but it was not the safest option. It's quick, cheap and desperate. I couldn't recommend it, and neither can the manufacturers – they're not meant to be used in enclosed spaces. But if you insist on using this kind of heater make sure it has a built in flame failure device and oxygen depletion sensor. And make sure there is enough ventilation in the van.

One example of this kind of gas heater is the 'Mr Buddy' portable heater. This is probably the safest out of all the gas heaters, but for the price you might as well get a proper forced air heater, like a Propex.

Propex heater

This is a type of blown air heater designed to safely heat small spaces like boats and camper vans. They run on gas (using your main gas supply) but also need a 12V supply to power the fan. It sucks air in and blows hot air out, heated by an enclosed gas burner inside. The unit is completely sealed and has a 'closed flue' which means it takes combustion air from outside of the living space and sends exhaust air outside. So there's no chance of dangerous gasses coming into your van and it won't use up the oxygen. They work very well and are often built into many new factory-built campers and motorhomes.

I installed one of these after two years of living in my van (search the blog for 'propex heater' to see photos of the installation). I bought it second hand (it's 23 years old) and installed it myself after fixing and servicing it. It provides instant heat and it warms up the whole van nicely in about 15 minutes. I installed it inside the bench at the back of my van where my desk is, so it's totally hidden. I'm sat here now, writing, whilst it warms my feet.

These heaters have an adjustable wall mounted thermostat so it will turn off when the van gets to the right temperature and turn on when it falls below the temperature. The only disadvantage of these is that the noise from the fan is enough to wake me up so I usually don't have it on during the night unless it's really cold.

Example: Propex HS2000

Diesel heater

These are similar in shape, size and functionality to the Propex heaters but use diesel instead of gas. They can be slightly more efficient than the gas Propex heaters but are more noisy and more difficult to fix if they go wrong. And depending on your van, they could be more difficult to install because you have to provide a supply of diesel to it, which could mean either installing a separate tank or tapping into the fuel tank of the van's engine.

Example: Eberspacher Airtronic and Webasto Air Top

Gas radiator

These are common in older factory-built motorhomes and caravans. They are mounted against a wall and use gas to heat up radiating elements inside. The advantage of these over the forced air type (like the Propex and diesel heaters above) is that they don't make any noise so you can have have it on during the night without it waking you up. Also, because these heaters have no moving parts, they are very reliable. And you can pick them up for less than £100 second hand.

Example: Trumatic S3002 Gas Heater

Vehicles you can live in

I'll go through some varieties of the liveable vehicles you might come across. Many of these terms overlap and definitions can differ depending on your country. For example, recreational vehicle (RV), motorhome and camper van could all be used to describe the same vehicle – any motor vehicle that is equipped with living space and amenities of a house. But in the UK, a motorhome is usually a larger and more complete version of a camper van. And to me, an 'RV' is more of an American name for a large coach-built motorhome, but still could be used to describe any vehicle that is 'recreational'.

Coach-built motorhome or RV

A coach-built motorhome is based on the bare chassis of a standard van or truck with the whole shell being custom made in a factory for the purpose of living – it's the classic motorhome look. They come with everything you'd find in a house including a full kitchen, toilet, shower and even a TV. Some of them are almost like actual houses. There are loads of different variations and sub-classes of motorhomes, but I won't go into that here.

In Europe, it's mostly older people driving these kinds of large motorhomes. So maybe this is the kind of thing to get if you've just retired and you want something comfortable, complete and with all the facilities of a house – and you have the money to spend. It is possible to get some older coach-built motorhomes (or RVs) second-hand for a fair price but they often need a fair bit of work doing on the body and interior.

Factory-built camper van or motorhome

These are usually smaller than a coach-built motorhome and are based on a standard van shell with the inside professionally converted into a living space. It will have all the features to live comfortably but maybe not as many as a coach-built - for example it may have a more basic kitchen and washing facilities.

The good thing about a factory-built camper van (as opposed to self-built) is that you can be sure it has been built to good standards with everything you need all ready to go. The disadvantage is the higher cost, although they're still much cheaper than a larger coach-built motorhome. Also, the materials to build the interior are usually chosen mainly for practical reasons over aesthetics. I'm yet to see a factory converted van that really feels like a warm cosy home but maybe that's down to taste.

Self-built camper van or motorhome

This is the same as the above (and may look exactly the same) but converted either by a previous owner or by you. If you have a good idea of how you want your van to be, and you have the time, then converting a van yourself could be a good option.

Some people may just want to put a camping bed and a portable cooker in an empty van and set off travelling. Others may want a shower, toilet and proper built-in kitchen. Converting a van yourself lets you focus on only the things that are important to you, potentially saving space and money. The nice thing is you can fully personalise it to make it your own and it's completely down to you and your imagination. And it's a rewarding feeling to live in something that you have built yourself.

It could also be worth considering a half-built van conversion or an unfinished project. Many people start a van conversion project and for whatever reason are not able to finish them. If you find a van with a basic layout that suits you, you can always change the colours and décor yourself and customise it how you want. eBay can be a good place to look for these – try searching with keywords like 'project van' or 'unfinished camper van project'.

For a full guide on van conversion (including costs, materials and everything else you need to know) see my other book: *From Van to Home – How I made an old rusty van into my cosy off-grid home*. You can get it here: vandogtraveller.com/van-conversion-book

Bus

They make great homes until you have to pay for the fuel. My neighbours right now (across the road, on the beach in Tarifa, Spain) live in a single decker 10m bus. It's a beautiful home and bigger than a flat in London – search the blog for 'Blue Bus' to get a tour. The downsides (although this depends on how you want to use it) are mostly practical points: you can't just park it up outside a shop whilst you get a loaf of bread.

But if you are living mostly in nature, moving only every few weeks or months, or if you are a family and you need the space, then it could be worth it. Although, if you go the wrong way down a narrow road you might have to drive for a long time before there's space to turn round – I've done three point turns on small mountain roads in my van and it's not nice.

Trucks, lorries and wagons

Usually used for cargo and freight, these kinds of vehicles have usually been well maintained and will probably have a lot of life left in them. You'll mostly find these at specialist auctions rather than ads in the local paper. With a truck or a lorry you are getting a huge rectangular space to do whatever you want with – or you might find one already converted.

You see many truck-homes used by the free-festival-people (the ones I mentioned earlier) for carrying sound systems and for living in. These people usually stay in the same place over winter and travel only in the spring and summer for the party season. But like a bus these can be difficult to drive around cities, and they are not so economical. And finding a camping spot is more difficult.

Specialist

Things like ambulances, fire trucks, horse boxes, military vehicles, vintage and utility vehicles. These vehicles have usually been well maintained throughout their life and kept in good condition. If you want something unique, this could be for you. But like with all older vehicles, you'll have to make sure that spare parts are still available.

Caravan (travel trailer)

It's easy to overlook the humble caravan – I think in the US you call them travel trailers. They do have some advantages over a van conversion. For one, you can disconnect your car to use it as normal and benefit from the better fuel economy. And if your engine catastrophically fails, you can just get a new car – your whole home doesn't rely on the working of an engine. The other advantage of a caravan is you can get an old second hand one for very cheap – people sometimes give them away. But I still prefer a van because it's all self contained and a little more discreet.

Other

It could be any kind of DIY contraption: a shed on the back of a pickup, a tent on a roof rack. The possibilities are endless. There's no vehicle you cannot live in.

Convert a van yourself or buy already converted?

Converting a van can be quite a long project if you've never done anything like it before. It doesn't require you to be an exceptionally skilled craftsman, electrician or plumber, but basic DIY skills definitely help. It can work out cheaper to convert a van yourself rather than buying one second hand, but it could also be more expensive if you don't keep a track of your costs. Convert a van yourself if:

- You have a good idea of how you want everything – layout, décor and features
- You want to customise it exactly how you want
- You want a unique layout to exactly fit your needs
- You cannot see any converted vans you like or that

would suit your needs
- You enjoy doing projects like this
- You have time – and you have time to go over your deadline, because it probably will

If you just want to go on a road trip for a few weeks or months then it may not be worth spending months converting a van yourself. Buy a van already converted if:

- You want to live in it as soon as possible and your time is limited
- You want something ready and complete without having to worry what needs to go into it, including all the technical stuff
- You don't enjoy making things
- You're not too bothered about having something that is fully personalised to your taste

I decided to convert a van myself because I had a clear picture in my head of how I wanted my van to be. And I thought that if I was going to spend this amount of money on a van that I should try and get it exactly how I wanted. It was a long process but I learnt a lot and I couldn't be happier with how it came out. It's still going strong after three years.

Choosing your van – things to consider

Whether you're converting a van yourself or not, the main consideration for most people, apart from cost, is probably the size. Once you have a rough idea of the kind of size you want – or rather, what you want to put in the space – you can have a look at some vans and then narrow it down to maybe one or two models.

For me, I decided I would get an LDV Convoy, because they are cheap, wide and just the right length and height for what I wanted. For the next few weeks, all I searched for was LDV

Convoys. I got to know this van well – the variations, price ranges and what would be considered good condition for a certain age.

Here are some things you may want to think about when choosing your van:

Do you want to live or camp?

If you want to live and/or travel for extended periods then a high top roof (i.e. being able to stand up), in my opinion, is a must and makes all the difference between a camper and a comfortable home that you can actually live in. It's quite a different experience – I don't think I could have lived for this long in a van that I couldn't stand up in. But I do know people who have lived in their small campers for years, and I guess it's something you can just get used to if needed.

How much time will you spend in your van?

If you'll be away from your van for most of the day you might just want somewhere to eat and sleep at night, in which case a small camper may work for you. On the other hand, you may want to spend more time in your van, in which case you'll want something bigger and probably something you can stand up in. My van is very much my home. I do all the normal things in there that I did in my house and I couldn't do that if I had a smaller camper.

How many people?

You need to think about bed space and also any extra space for guests. Maybe you'll have one permanent bed that can sleep two and one guest bed that folds out or is made using existing surfaces in the van – like from the seating. You might also want to consider potential room for expansion, just in case. In my van I can comfortably sleep two, uncomfortably sleep three and very uncomfortably sleep four – two people in the bed, one in the hammock and one across the front seats.

Do you need room for any of your sports or hobbies?

This can take up a lot of room. You may even decide to build your van around the storage of all your gear. I met a guy the other day in Portugal and most of the space in his van was taken up by his collection of surfboards. I guess it depends how much you love your sport. But if you don't have much room inside the van, a roof rack is useful.

Will you be doing a lot of travelling?

If you plan on travelling a lot, fuel economy might be more important to you. You're never going to get amazing fuel economy when your home is on wheels, but that's the compromise you have to make. If you want to travel around slowly, or just move south for winter, then fuel economy might not be as much of a priority.

City or countryside?

The bigger the vehicle the more difficult it is to navigate around big cities and also to park up and manoeuvre. When choosing my van I wanted to find a balance – a van that was big enough for living but not too big to drive in the city.

What kind of licence do you have?

In the UK 3.5 tonnes is the maximum vehicle weight you can drive on a normal licence. If you want to get something bigger than 3.5 tonnes you might have to get a heavy vehicle license - unless you got your licence before 1997, in which case you don't need to take an extra test and you can drive up to 8.2 tonnes. This is something you'd have to check depending on your country.

Freecamping or campsites?

Some people only stay on campsites, others will only freecamp and some people might do a mixture of both. This might affect what facilities you decide to have in your van. If you'll be staying on campsites, you can comfortably live with very minimal facilities on board. If you plan on mostly freecamping you'll want to be as autonomous as possible with solar panels for electricity and enough storage for water and gas. My plan was to only freecamp so I built my van with this in mind.

Are spare parts easily available?

If you get some strange imported van or a vintage fire truck – or my van – you may have difficulty finding spare parts, which can be time consuming and very expensive. So getting a van that has spare parts widely available in the countries you'll be using it in is important.

What van to convert yourself?

There is no 'best van' to convert. It depends on you, your requirements and how you want to use it. Generally speaking, the best van would be one that is mechanically sound and is the right size for your needs.

You can convert pretty much any vehicle into your home. Most people choose a standard commercial van as a base vehicle since they are common and easy to get to get hold of. These are mainly designed for tradesmen and utility companies for the purpose of running their business and transporting goods. In the UK we call these panel vans, light good vehicles or just 'white vans'. For example, the Ford Transit, Mercedes Sprinter or Iveco Daily.

Most panel vans come in different lengths – referred to as the wheelbase, which is the distance between the front and back wheels. You may see LWB (long wheel base) or XLWB (extra long wheel base) and even XXL for the new sprinters –

they're big. There's no strict size guide though and all manufacturers have their own idea of what makes something a LWB – it is relative to that particular model. When researching your van, you should look at what wheelbase lengths are available for the model you're interested in. It's a good idea to go and have a look at some vans in real life (inside and out) to get an idea of what they mean by standard or long wheelbase.

Panel vans can come with or without a 'high top'. This is usually a fibreglass moulded (but can also be metal) top that is factory made to extend the roof upwards to give more head room. An average sized person (just under 6ft) will probably just be able to stand up inside a high top van. Some vans only come in a high top version, like the Mercedes Sprinter, whilst others may come as a high top or standard height. But don't assume that just because it's a high top you can stand up in it. It may be worth standing in a few different high top vans to see how much they can differ.

Some panel vans might also come as a variation, called a 'Luton van' or just a 'Luton' - or 'box van' in the US. These are often based on the same chassis as a normal van, but with a larger boxy space that's usually made of a lightweight plastic, rather than steel. They're often used by home removal companies and will usually have a large shutter at the back for loading and unloading goods. The advantage of a Luton is that it gives you a nice big square space to convert, making it easier to work with – as opposed to the curved profile walls of normal vans. Also, you get a lot more headroom in a Luton, so it could be worth considering if you're really tall, or you want to have bunk beds – or for a mezzanine with a library and sliding ladders.

Then there are all the smaller vans that are usually classed as small campers or weekend campers. For example, the VW camper or Toyota Hiace. Like I mentioned earlier, to me this is more camping than living, but it all depends on what you're doing.

How much does a van cost?

There is no straight answer. There's too much variation and it depends on what you want. The best way to answer this question is to research what vans might suit your needs and have a look at how much they are selling for on eBay. My van cost £2500 and another £2800 to convert (repairs included). A total of £5400. Here are some of the factors that will affect the price of your van:

- **Make.** A VW or Mercedes would usually cost more than a Ford. Some manufacturers just seem to have a good reputation and are able to hold their value more than others.
- **Mileage.** As with all vehicles, the more mileage the engine has done the less it sells for. But this can be used to our advantage when buying a van (assuming it's diesel). A well looked after diesel engine can do hundreds of thousands of miles in its lifetime and low mileage is not so important when compared with a petrol engine.
- **General Condition.** Any signs of rust will make for a cheaper sale, but you have to be careful because it could end up costing you a lot more in the long run. Rust can completely destroy a vehicle and bodywork repair is time-consuming and can end up costing a lot.
- **Age.** The value of any vehicle depreciates the most in the first few years, so it's usually more cost effective to get something that's at least five years old.
- **Service history.** A full service history is worth a lot because you can be sure the engine has been looked after, and so you can expect the price to be a bit higher.

- **Previous owners.** The kind of previous owner can make a difference to the price. Most people would rather buy a van that has been used by the local church rather than a typical 'white van' man. I don't know why.
- **Size.** Biggest is not always the most expensive. Sometimes it's the opposite. Bigger vans are more difficult to keep and people usually want to get rid of them as soon as possible – like buses, horse boxes and trucks. Also, bigger vehicles might require a heavy goods licence which not everyone has, so it makes it more difficult to sell and therefore lowers the price.
- **Recent work done.** If the van has had any work done to it like a new clutch, tyres, belts or anything that has been fixed recently it can make for a higher sale price. But it could save you time and money in the long run.

I recommend leaving some money aside for repairs and renovation – about £1000 is probably a safe bet. There's always something that needs doing.

Before you hand the money over

If you've found a van you like, there are some things you should check before you part with your money. That's what I'll go through now.

Does it suit your needs?

If the van only half suits your needs and it looks like it has some potential problems, move on to the next one. It's probably not worth fixing and there will be better options out there for you. If the van does have everything you're looking for but has a few problems, it still might be worth buying. Problems can be fixed. So if the van is perfect in all other areas, don't let it totally put you off.

Quality of work (if buying a self-converted van)

If you're buying a van that has been converted by someone else, you should check the quality of work inside the living space. It might have loads of features that sound good on the advert but if the work is of poor quality it might not last very long and it might be unsafe. You don't want to have to spend more money later down the line because bad work has been done on the van.

The things that I'd mainly be concerned with are the electronics and the gas system. In the UK there are no regulations for installing electronics and gas appliances into vehicles, which means anyone can do this kind of work and potentially cause some problems if corners have been cut. Someone with basic DIY experience should be able to inspect the quality of the work and spot any clues that would indicate poor workmanship or incompetence. If in doubt, bring a handy friend with you to help you check it out.

Vehicle specific faults

As vehicles age they may develop their own specific faults. On my van the dual mass flywheel fails after about 100k miles. It also has a problem with the ECU (engine control unit) getting water damaged because of a leaking windscreen seal. When I was buying my van I was aware of these things (after a Google search) and knew what to check. It's always worth investigating these problems before you buy.

Mileage

As I mentioned, high mileage on the clock of a diesel van needn't be a deal breaker. Mileage is not always a direct indication of engine condition for a diesel engine. What's just as important (maybe more) is how those miles were clocked up. For example, a van that has mostly been used for long distance trips that has 100k miles on the clock is quite likely to have a better condition engine than one with 50k miles that has only ever been driven in the city. Diesel engines are designed to be used for long periods at a time, otherwise unburnt carbon deposits can build up and cause problems. This is why some adverts might describe the van as having 'motorway miles'.

If a diesel engine is well looked after it will run for hundreds of thousands of miles. I met a guy recently who had over 1 million miles on his Ford Transit camper van. And he sees no reason why it shouldn't keep on running.

Rust, body work and structural integrity

Before buying your van, you should thoroughly check for rust. Most vans more than a few years old will probably have some signs of rust – especially in the UK where the climate is damp. Common problem areas are around the roof guttering, wheel arches, and bottom of doors. In my experience, whenever there are visible signs of rust showing on the body, there's usually a lot more hidden underneath. A bit of light rust is easy to deal with but more severe rust can cost a lot in welding repairs. You can check for rust by getting under the van with a torch and using a screwdriver to tap or chip away at rusted areas to check the severity. It could be useful to categorise rust into three categories (this isn't official, I just made it up):

1. **Surface rust.** This kind of rust is not a problem and you can easily treat and remove it yourself using rust remover and some paint. If you only have surface rust then you're lucky – it will not have affected the integrity of the metal – but it should be treated right away before it gets worse.
2. **Rust that causes the metal to be heavily pitted.** This level of rust will have permanently deformed the metal surface and possibly weakened it. It might sound a bit different to the other non-rusted areas

when tapped with a screwdriver. Often you can save these areas (fully removing the rust and painting as above) as long as it hasn't compromised the structural integrity of the van – it's always worth getting a second opinion on this.

3. **Rust that has penetrated right through the metal.** With rust like this the screwdriver will go straight through the metal and leave red dust in its place. That's when you're going to need some welding doing.

Bits of rust here and there on the body are relatively easy to deal with, but if there's severe rust (category three) on parts of the chassis, I'd stay away. In the 'Van maintenance & problems' chapter I'll go over how to treat non-severe rust and how to protect your van so it'll last for years to come.

Check the engine and mechanics

There are several checks that you can do yourself when looking at a potential van to buy – before you hand the money over. Of course, it's difficult to thoroughly check everything and even after passing these checks there is still a level of trust between you and the seller. If you feel you can't trust the seller then you're probably right.

Start engine from cold

It should start straight away after no more than a few turns of the engine. You shouldn't have to give it any gas and it should settle to a steady and consistent idle. If the seller has warmed the engine up before you come to look at it ask him why.

I learnt my lesson with this. When I went to look at my van, the owner had the engine already warmed up and idling. I later realised (after I bought it) he was hiding a problem he didn't want me to see. If I'd have known to start the engine from cold I would have been able to catch him out and have it repaired before I bought it. At least you can learn from my mistake.

Listen

Diesels engines do sound a lot louder and clunkier than petrol engines, but any unusual sounds can indicate a problem – loud tapping, knocking or whirring. The engine should sound consistent and relatively smooth.

Test drive

Take the van for a drive and get up to a decent speed. There should be no loss of power or hesitation and gears should change easily and smoothly. Also check the general handling including braking, unusual vibrations and steering.

Look at the exhaust

The Exhaust smoke can give clues to many problems on a diesel engine – I'll mention some of them later in the maintenance chapter. A very light black smoke is normal on a diesel but it shouldn't consistently kick out black sooty smoke. There may be a little bit of sooty smoke when you first start the engine or when you accelerate hard (especially before the engine has warmed up) but that's usually normal. White/blue smoke is also not a good sign and often indicates a worse problem than black smoke.

Check oil

Check the oil by looking at the inside of the oil cap. It will probably be black and dirty, which is quite normal, but it shouldn't be foamy and it shouldn't have any white or milky appearance. Contaminated oil like this could indicate some internal engine problem or leak.

Check coolant

There should be no signs of anything else in the coolant tank, like oil, fuel or the smell of exhaust. And the coolant should be a consistent colour with no gunk or solid matter floating around. Also, any bubbles in the expansion tank (whilst the engine is running) means air is getting in from somewhere in the coolant system, which would indicate a leak.

Check for leaks

Inspect the engine for any signs of oil or fluid leaks. If something is too clean, or there are signs of a leak being recently wiped up with a cloth, I'd ask questions. Also look for puddles or oil stains on the floor where the van has been kept.

Fault lights

A warning light on the dash could indicate anything from a simple blown fuse to something much more costly and complicated. If you see a fault light, you could look up on the internet what the possible causes could be.

When to be wary of buying

Do you have a bad feeling about the seller? Does he have loads of other vehicles on his driveway? Is he selling for a 'friend'? Did he want to meet you in a carpark and not at his home? Does he seem eager to get rid of it, or insists that he drops the van off at your house asap? Does he seem uneasy about you having a mechanic or friend check it over? To me, these things would raise suspicions.

Private or from a dealer?

In the UK, there are virtually no consumer rights if you buy a vehicle privately. So it's up to you to fully inspect the vehicle before you hand the money over, which can make buying a van privately a bit of a gamble. A van bought from a dealer might cost a bit more but it could be worth it because of the guarantee you get, even if it's just for one month.

Get a mechanic to check it over

If you've decided you want the van, and you've done some of the checks I've just talked about, don't part with you money until you get a second opinion. Either find a friend or pay a mechanic to come with you and check the van out. Explain to the seller you can give a deposit now, paying the full amount after the mechanic says it's all good. An honest seller should have no problem with this.

Having a mechanic check over my van before I bought it is something I wish I did, and for £50 or so it would have been worth it. An experienced mechanic will know the things that go wrong with that particular make of van and will be able to advise how much any repairs would cost, helping you make a better decision about whether to buy or not.

How I chose my van

I bought an LDV Convoy LWB high top with a 2.4 Diesel injection engine. It was made in 2003 but the design is based on something much older (the Leyland Sherpa). To drive, it definitely feels like an old van. It does a maximum speed of 60mph (although, you wouldn't want to go that fast) and handles corners like… well, it doesn't really handle corners. But I like it. Here's why I chose this van:

- It's white and generic looking – blends into the city landscape
- It's high enough to stand up in – I'm 5ft 11"
- The engine is a Ford and parts are widely available
- It's fairly wide (2m across the floor)
- It's just long enough for a comfortable living space but not too long to drive and park
- It's very simply built and has very basic features – less things to go wrong and easier to fix

I probably could have chosen a better van for travelling Europe. These vans were made in England and the company went bust in 2006 so parts can be difficult to find in England, let alone Europe. But I'm lucky that the engine is Ford, so engine parts are available worldwide. But if I need a body part, or anything other than an engine part, I have to get it from the UK – and usually from a scrapyard.

Saying that, the van has been solid and reliable. It's taken me thousands of miles through some tough mountains and bumpy backroads and nothing major has gone wrong in the three years I've had it. So I'm happy.

5

Prepare for take off

In this chapter I'll go through some things you'll need to do to get ready for your adventure on the road. Everyone reading this book will be in different situations or at different stages but I'll share the things I did to prepare for my journey, and some things that I would do in hindsight. From this point on I'll assume you have your van pretty much ready to live in.

Telling people

If you suddenly tell your family that you are moving out of your house, selling most your stuff and moving into a van, they might worry. Ease them into it if you think it might help.

Sometimes I get asked what my friends and family thought when I told them I was quitting my job to live in a van and travel. I'd say I got three different kinds of reactions:

1. **'How are you going to do that?** You can't do that. You need a job.' Maybe these people wish they could do the same but they've convinced themselves it's not possible. Take what they say with a big pinch of salt.
2. **'But you have a great job.'** Older people might say stuff like this. But times have changed. There are different options now.
3. **'Excellent have fun. I want to do that. Can I come with you?'** Keep these people close. Hang around with them, let them help you, bring them along and get them on board. Chances are these people are already your good friends.

Before you tell your family, coworkers and manager, it's a good idea to tell at least one person who will understand and support what you're doing – especially if you're doing this whole thing on your own. I don't mean someone who just pretends to understand, but someone who thinks it's a great idea and who you can talk with about your plans. It's probably one of your good friends or someone you share similar views with. You need that person for support and to back you up when you, and others, start questioning your sanity.

How much money do you need?

It depends on many things: your personal habits and lifestyle, what you'll be doing, how you want to live, how much travelling you want to do and in what countries.

Some people will be more willing than others to compromise certain comforts and luxuries. Our comfort levels are all different and we all have a different idea of what is absolutely necessary and what isn't. I don't mind wearing the same clothes every day and I don't mind getting food out of bins if I have to. I don't do that anymore but I did in my first year when money was running low, before I worked things out. I still wear the same clothes though.

One thing is for sure: the more money you have the more you will spend. If you have only a few pounds a day to travel on, that's all you'll spend. If you have hundreds of pounds a day, you will spend much more. So I have no idea how much money you'll need. I'll just share with you what I did.

Budgeting

I'd never lived in a van or travelled before and trying to come up with a budget seemed difficult. So my aim was just to travel for as long as possible whilst spending as little as possible. After spending £5500 on my van, I had £4500 left over for travelling with – or about €5300. I felt like this was enough to set me off in a direction, and that it would give me enough time to work out ways to extend or sustain my journey.

You might already have a way, or ideas, to make money whilst you're on the road. Whether it's busking on the streets or running your current business remotely. But it's still a good idea to have some money as a buffer to get you started and to give you room for adjustments and experimentation.

If you want to work out an exact budget for each day it might be best to first spend some time in your van, because the costs are different, and a lot less, than living in a house. After a couple of weeks or months you'll probably have a good idea of what you'll spend. Also, it could be helpful to work out how long certain amounts of money would last you. For example, the €5300 I saved up would last six months spending €30 a day, or one year spending around €15 a day, or two years spending €7.50 a day.

If at any point in your journey you realise you're running low on money or if you want to stretch your money a bit further you can always stop for a while to do some easy and simple work. It could be picking fruit, working on a farm or offering to help people on Workaway in exchange for food – this kind of work is always available.

My friend, Finn (he's on the blog), travelled Europe for six months with no money. He travelled with his £60 guitar and made money as he needed it. Instead of going to the cash machine he'd go into the nearest town centre and play a few classical pieces for a couple of hours. He makes money and he makes people happy.

I'll talk more later about making money in the chapter 'Making money on the road'. But now I'll go over some of the main costs. For me, and probably for most people, the main expense is food and diesel.

Food
The cost of food can vary hugely from person to person and personal habits will affect your budget a lot. Eating meat and drinking alcohol every day is expensive. Being good at cooking (or just being willing to cook every day) can help you make decent healthy meals for cheap. I still cook and prepare food (breakfast, lunch and dinner) every day in my van. But every now and then I'll eat out.

But during my first year I didn't buy one meal out, and I didn't buy any meat. It was too expensive. Now I realise how much of a luxury meat is and how unnecessary it is to have it every single day, or even every other day. Or even at all – it saves money and it's better for the animals and the planet.

One time, me and Finn were living in a remote valley in the Hungarian countryside. I was coming to the end of my money and all Finn had was the loose change in his guitar case. The only thing we spent money on were vegetables and food from a local farmers stall. We spent less than €10 per week between us but we were still able to have big feasts every day with all different kinds of good food. That month cost us €20 each and we lived so well. We had food and we had music. There was nothing else we needed.

Nowadays I spend about €30 per week on shopping – although it can be a lot less depending on the country. I'll talk a bit more about food and cooking in a van later on in the chapter 'Cooking & eating'.

Diesel

If you want to travel, the cost of fuel is an unavoidable expense, although you can do some things to reduce it. The cost of diesel will depend on:

- **The country.** 1L of diesel in the UK is equivalent to about €1.50 whereas in Morocco it's €0.75.
- **Economy of your engine.** American vehicles seem to be a lot less efficient than those in Europe, often less than half the MPG.
- **How many people are sharing the cost.** Sharing fuel costs helps a lot. If you're travelling alone you can use car sharing sites or find a travel partner for a few days, weeks or months.
- **How much travelling you'll be doing.** I travel very slowly and don't make any big jumps across countries. If I've done a lot of travelling in the previous weeks I'll ease back a bit to average it out. Sometimes, when I find a nice place or nice people, I won't move for weeks or months.

Alternative fuels

If you have a diesel engine, you can use vegetable oil as an alternative fuel. I've met many people travelling Europe on vegetable oil – some using 100% vegetable oil and some using a mixture of oil and diesel. There are many ways to do this and there are different oils you can use, ranging from recycled chip pan oil to virgin vegetable oil pressed specifically to run in an engine.

If you are interested in supplementing your diesel with cooking oil, research as much as you can about it. You'll usually have to do a couple of simple modifications to the van, depending on your engine and the climate you'll be driving in. With the right research and engine modifications you can run your engine problem free.

But I don't do this. Some engines don't work well with vegetable oil and mine's one of them.

Van running costs

These are things like vehicle insurance, vehicle tax, repair and maintenance costs for the van. With tax and insurance it's often cheaper if you pay for the whole year in full, rather than on a month by month basis. Also, in the UK you might get cheaper insurance if your van is officially registered as a motor caravan.

As for repairs, you may go for a whole year with no mechanical problems, not having to spend anything, but the next year you might get several things go wrong. So you'll need to keep some money to the side for this – I mentioned earlier that about £1k would be a safe bet. With my van the problems seem to come all at once and then it's fine for maybe another year. It can be painful to spend a load of money at once on repairs but it averages out over time, and it's just part of owning a van. If you're already mechanically minded or are willing to get your hands a bit oily, this is where you can save a lot of money on garage bills.

Leisure

I see leisure costs as anything else that isn't totally essential to your survival and travels. Things like hobbies, activities and buying ice creams.

You might have to make some slight adjustments or compromises when it comes to these kinds of expenses. My friend jumps out of planes for his hobby and it's really expensive. He often has to choose between that and travelling. But he recently thought of a solution: buy his own parachute rig so he can jump off things for free whenever he feels like it.

Most of the things I do for fun don't cost much – that is, once I've bought the stuff to do it. But when summer comes I like to go to festivals and they can cost a fair bit.

But sometimes you can just make things happen. During my first summer on the road, in Hungary, we had no money to go to the Ozora festival. We spent two days trying to raise money by selling cakes and playing music at the entrance. We finally got the money but we got sold fake tickets, so we lost it all. The next option was to sneak in, crawling through the wet corn fields for 45 minutes. We got caught. But then the owner of the festival came and bought us all tickets because he admired our persistence. I went to four festivals that summer. I didn't pay for one.

How much do I spend travelling Europe in my van?

During my first year travelling Europe I spent, on average, just under €12 per day – about €4300. That's including diesel, food, van insurance, tax and everything that came out my bank account in that 12 months. To be exact, it was €5.64 per day for fuel and €6.11 per day for living and everything else – including van tax and insurance. Even if I had a planned budget, I probably wouldn't have been able to spend less. I tried hard to make this last. Being a student was nothing compared to this. I wouldn't even spend 20 cents on a sponge to wash the dishes.

I've met people who do it for cheaper, but like I said earlier, there's a point where it comes down to the limit of your personal comfort. For me, even though some days I wouldn't spend anything, €12 daily average was probably the lowest I could manage whilst still having an amazing time, eating well and not being too uncomfortable. I saw it as a challenge most of the time and it became a bit of a game. And because I was travelling and having a great time, I never felt like I needed anything more.

I learnt that having little money made no difference to my happiness or quality of life. My happiness and quality of life actually increased. All of my favourite and most memorable experiences didn't cost a thing. I'll talk more about how to spend as little money as possible in the 'Travelling happy' chapter later on.

After my first year of travel I spent more. I started to make some money online so I reinvested some back into myself and the blog – I bought a decent camera, books and things that would help me improve and carry on what I was doing. I also travelled a lot more and started to live more luxuriously, buying organic peanut butter, blueberries and the odd meal out. Right now I'm living on about €400 per month without too many worries.

Example of spending

Here's a hypothetical budget that is loosely based on my experience. I feel that, at least for me, this would be a reasonable and attainable budget – it's not as tight as my first year's spending.

	Daily average (€)	Weekly average (€)	Monthly average (€)	Yearly average (€)
Food	6	42	168	2016
Diesel/ fuel	7	49	196	2352
Running costs	2.50	17	66	800
Leisure	3	21	84	1020
Total	€18.50	€129	€514	€6188

Some tips on saving up

I met a couple in a pub in my home town. They'd been living in the carpark, in their van, for six months to help them save money for travelling. They both kept their normal jobs and managed to save up faster than ever. They're now in Portugal for winter in their big red truck-home.

But saving money up isn't easy. The more we earn the more we spend and it's a difficult law to defy. There are hundreds of books dedicated to the subject of saving money but I'll share some simple things that helped me:

- **Keep your goal and vision in your mind every day.** Think about this when you first wake up in the morning and when you go to bed at night.
- **Focus on the reason you are saving the money.** When working offshore I was constantly thinking about why I was doing the work, which helped keep me motivated. In my spare time, I'd be on the computer researching vans and creating my blog. I was the weirdo who didn't watch films or play games

with the other workers in the couple of hours off at the end of the day. I was focused. It's worth it in the end.

- **Look for extra opportunities at your work.** I started to work overtime in the evenings and on weekends. I also put myself forward to do more work on oil rigs, sometimes working over 70 hours per week in the North Sea.
- **Find other streams of income.** If there are no extra opportunities in your current job, get another job or make some money on the side using some of your skills – this could also be helpful for later when you're on the road.
- **Create a savings account.** Every month you can move money into this account leaving only the very minimum you need for living in your main account. It sounds simple but it works well and it stops you from spending more than you need to.
- **Question yourself before you buy big things.** Do you really need that? If you really need a car, you just need something that works, nothing more. Or just buy a bike and cycle everywhere.
- **Record and review your expenses.** And cut out any expensive habits and luxuries.

The thing is, we can always do with more money, but we have to cut it off somewhere and trust that other opportunities will come up, because they probably will. So I think it's good to decide how much money you'll need first, setting that as a goal and sticking to it. This is what I talk about now.

Quit the job

I felt a lot of resistance when I was quitting my job – from myself and the people around me. Doing the opposite to everyone can be difficult to do. Believing in yourself is difficult to do. I was doubting myself a lot. Everyone was asking me the same questions I'd been asking myself over and over. I was having those kinds of dreams where I'd be walking up a flight of stairs in the opposite direction against huge crowds and not getting anywhere. Quitting a job is difficult.

Knowing what I know now, there are many things that I'd go back and tell myself if I could. Here are some of them:

- You can come back to this world (the world of conventional jobs, offices and the nine-to-five life) whenever you like. It's always there.
- We are not designed to sit in an office with no sunlight and look at screens for eight hours a day.
- A job should be used to sustain the life you want. Not the other way round. Or you can use your job as a springboard into a direction that excites you – your next adventure.
- When you quit, your mind will be more free and creative to think of fresh ideas and different options. Your brain will shift into a new gear.
- Quitting your job is not giving up. Nor is it failing. You are taking a proactive step in a direction in order to create the life you want.
- People's advice is often tainted with their own fears. Be careful about taking advice from scared people, including yourself.
- You don't have to know all the answers. You don't always need a solid fool-proof plan and you don't need to have the answers to everyone's questions. It's OK to say 'I don't know…yet'.

How to quit your job in four steps

It's tempting to just get up from your desk, get in your van and leave forever. You might daydream about all the different ways you can quit. But it's probably best to do it nicely – and no tipping desks as you walk out.

For months I was saying to friends I was going to quit my job. They got sick of hearing it and I got sick of thinking about it. I realised I was putting it off, making excuses and resisting it. The problem was, I didn't know how to quit. They teach you how to get a job but not how to quit. Part of the problem was knowing when to quit. There never seemed like a good time to do it. What I needed was an aim and a target. So I came up with these four steps to quitting a job. Maybe it will help you too.

1. Figure out your goals

What do you want to take from your job? It could be an amount of money or a specific skill. Or maybe you want to get a steady income from a side business before you quit your full time job.

I wanted to get to at least £10k because I thought this would be enough – £5k for the van and £5k for travelling. There wasn't much logic behind it. it was just a round number and it seemed like it would be enough. But whatever goal you set, make it specific.

2. Set a target date

Figure out the date when you expect to reach your goal and hand in your notice on that date. Put it in your calendar. Focus on that date. There is never a good time to leave your job. It will always be tricky and you will always be in the middle of projects. I messed up a couple of big projects at work before I quit but that's how it is. All you can do is carry on doing a good job right up to your last day. It's not your fault you want to be free.

I planned all stuff like this on my calendar with the prefix 'Project Vandog' – my secret project.

3. Quit

I decided to hand in my notice on a Friday to let it settle in over the weekend. We agreed on an official leaving date and I asked to be paid for the remaining holidays that I had not taken.

Note: you may get offered a pay rise, a bonus, an extended holiday or anything to keep you. Companies spend thousands finding and recruiting new people. They would rather you stay, and it is the job of the manager to keep you (even if deep down they understand your decision and wish they did the same years ago), so watch out.

You might be doubting yourself like crazy at this point and you might be thinking that this just wasn't meant to be. This is hard enough to deal with without people telling you that you're crazy and stupid for quitting your job, which brings us to the last and maybe most important step.

4. Get support and stay focused

Stay focused on what you want. Say no to everything else around you if it doesn't help you with your dream of travelling and living the van life – or whatever it is. This is when the friends who really understand you can help. And be careful of taking advice from people who don't understand or who have never done what you are trying to do.

You might feel totally out of your comfort zone and in a state of 'what have I done?'. Use this energy to put your plan into action. You'll work it out.

How to get rid of stuff

Living in a van is minimal living. But by minimal I don't mean living in a bare van with just a handful of possessions. I just mean having only the things you need. It's living efficiently and sensibly. In my van, everything has to earn its place. If it is not useful or has no sentimental value then it's gone. I've had to learn to be brutal with this otherwise I'd have no space and it would be difficult to live in.

So if you don't use all those knifes in that 20 piece kitchen knife set you got for Christmas, don't bring them all. I have one good sharp knife and that's all the knives I need. The same goes for all those kitchen utensils. You probably have a draw full of them in your house. You don't need them all. And all those coffee mugs. One per person. You only need what you need.

Shedding possessions might be an uncomfortable process at first but it doesn't have to result in living uncomfortably. Later down the line you'll probably see how nice it is to only have what you need, and to not be tied down by a ton of stuff that you'll never need or use.

And I probably don't need to say this but now is a good time to stop buying stuff you don't need – including the endless amount of travel gadgets that are available, and that you'll probably never use. You'll save money and precious van space. If you want to buy anything new, wait until you've sorted through all your things.

Here are ten tips for stripping down possessions:

1. Start now
It's best you start this shedding process as soon as possible. You might be a bit overwhelmed at the thought of having to get rid of all your stuff. Just take it one bit at a time, or one room at a time. Don't do as I did and leave it all for one weekend.

2. Sort into three piles: don't need, not sure and keep
Question everything. Do you really need that? Do you love it?

Will it make you money? It's easy to kid ourselves into keeping things but you have to catch yourself out and be realistic.

3. Tackle the not sure pile

If you're in two minds whether you should get rid of something or if you're worried you'll regret it, try putting it out of the way in a box somewhere for a month and see if you miss it. This will also help you lose attachment to it and will help you make a better decision whether it's worth keeping or not. You might think you'll miss it at first but more often than not, you won't.

4. You'll never read that pile of magazines

Even most charity shops wont take them. It's all available online anyway. Recycle them.

5. Get rid of all those clothes you don't wear

They might look nice but if you never wear them there's no point keeping them. Take them to a charity shop.

6. Digitise and scan any important documents

This includes receipts and documents that are still valid in digital form. I use the Evernote app which is great for scanning and storing documents. It lets you organise everything with tags and categories and it's all stored in the cloud so you can access your account from any computer or device, no matter where you are in the world.

7. Have ebooks instead of books

Some books you might still want to keep as a hard copy but the rest you can either recycle or give to a charity shop. I still have a bookshelf in my van because I have several books that I like to refer to often. But most of my books are now electronic.

8. Have your DVD collection in the cloud or on a hard

drive

For about £60 you can buy a 2TB hard drive to store all your DVDs. You can also sign up to video on demand services like Netflix or Amazon Prime. Although it's probably better to just store everything on a hard drive because streaming video requires a lot of internet bandwidth, which can be expensive when travelling.

9. Digitise all photos

If you have a load of old photo albums you can scan each photo using a high quality scanner to store and organise them all digitally on a computer.

10. Have a friend help you

They won't have the same emotional attachment as you do and they'll tell you when you have stupid reasons for keeping things.

Here's what to do with the things you don't need:

- **Sell it.** It's best to tackle this one first because it takes the longest. Use local ads, eBay, Gumtree or whatever.
- **Give it away or lend to someone.** You can advertise it online, putting 'FREE' in the title. Or you can just put it outside your house with a sign saying 'FREE'. If you really don't want to get rid of something, or you're not sure, you can lend it to friends and family.
- **Store it.** Paid storage is secure and safe but it's expensive. It's a last resort. It's best first to check with friends and family if they have any spare space in the attic or cellar.
- **Throw it away, recycle it, burn it.** If you can't do any of the above (or you have no time), invite all your friends round and have a party and a fire. Get them to bring their stuff too. Burn it. It'll be fun.

The next bit is about packing your van. If you still have too much stuff you'll have to go back to this section – you might have to do that a few times.

Packing the van

A good way to start packing is to get all the things you want to bring and lay them out on the floor – outside next to the van would be good. This will give you an idea of how much room things take up, and seeing it all at once will give you a better idea of how much of it there actually is. Once you have all your stuff in front of you, question if it's worth the space it takes up (again). Do you really need that? You'll be much happier with less stuff, I promise. You can tick it off your list as you put it in the van. But that's not what I did. I'm not that organised.

I have a friend who takes a pair of shorts for every day he is away on holiday. He says it's because he likes to have the option. Personally I hate having the option. I like to have hardly any clothes so I don't need to decide what to wear every single day. There are enough options as it is. But that's another example where we're all different.

I'm not going to write an extensive list of what to bring with you in your van because it probably wouldn't apply to everyone. Instead I'll go through the main categories and some of the essentials I have with me in my van. You can use this for ideas, and maybe as a start for your own list.

Note: I made a PDF checklist with all the stuff I'm about to go through. I also included some extra blank spaces for you to fill in with your own items. You can download it at vandogtraveller.com/van-checklist

Clothes

I bring enough clothes for a week: two pairs of jeans, a few tshirts, pants and a pair of shorts for the summer. For footwear I have a pair of trainers, boots and some flip-flops.

No matter where you'll be travelling, bring some warm clothes. One good warm jacket should be fine. It doesn't have to be full of special technology and all that patented fabric stuff. Just a warm jacket. I have a coat made from goats wool. It's about 40 years old. I found it in my dad's wardrobe. It's quite big and difficult to store but it's the warmest jacket I've ever had and I don't need much more when it gets cold.

Electronics

- **Wires and cables:** mini USB, micro USB, audio cables – paying more for good quality cables is well worth it in my experience
- Chargers – these are easy to forget
- **Camera –** I'll talk a bit more about my camera in the 'Entertainment & technology' chapter
- **iPod –** I use this for playing music in the cab and in the living space of my van
- **Portable speaker –** good for having music outside the van
- **Computer –** I have a 13" MacBook Pro
- **External hard drives:** for storing photos, films and backing up my computer
- **Headphones –** I have a pair of HD-25s which are almost indestructible and sound great
- **GPS –** I use a Garmin Nuvi-50 which I'll talk about in the next chapter

Leisure

I'll talk a bit more about some of this stuff in the later chapter, 'Entertainment & technology. It's something that will vary a lot for everyone but here's what I have:

- **Bicycle –** for getting around, exercising and doing

shopping
- **Slackline** – it's a nice activity to do in nature or in city parks
- **Inflatable boat** – for canals, rivers and lakes
- **Guitar** – even though I might not be very good, it's essential
- **Several other instruments and music toys** – like guitar, endless fun and learning
- **Pens, paper and stationery things** – so I can fill the wall of my van with notes, ideas and drawings
- **Books and Kindle** – most of my books are now electronic but I still have a bookshelf in the van

General van living

- **Kitchen equipment** – I'll list the essential cooking equipment in the 'Cooking & eating' chapter
- **Portable gas cooker:** for cooking outside
- **Hose pipe and connectors:** for filling up my water tank
- **LPG adaptors:** for filling my gas bottle in different countries
- **Camping furniture:** two camping chairs and a fold-up table
- **Large plastic woven ground matt**
- **A good blanket**
- **Hot water bottle** – these things are really great and combined with a good sleeping bag will keep you warm for most of the night
- **Sleeping bag** – I have a four season sleeping bag (Coleman Hudson 450), it's an XL size sleeping bag which I find much more comfortable and less claustrophobic than a regular size bag
- **Washbag and toiletries**
- **Washing line and pegs:** for drying clothes
- **Bucket:** for washing clothes

Tools

- **A basic tool kit.** Make sure that includes a full set of spanners – I prefer a socket set to individual open ended spanners because it takes up less room and it's easier to use. If your van has any odd or non-standard fittings that require specialised tools, bring these.
- **Wheel brace for changing wheels.** Make sure you've tested it out on your van and you can use it to change your wheel. A wheel brace for a car might not be long enough or strong enough for a van. And get a good quality one – I've snapped several.
- **Jack for changing wheels.** Get a decent one that has an adequate lift rating. Car jacks (like the scissor type) are usually rated at one or two tonne and are not strong enough for a van. I have a five tonne bottle-jack that works great.
- **Tow strap.** I use my slackline that can easily take several tonnes of load.
- **Jump leads.**

Spare parts

There's no need to bring as many spare parts as you can. If your van is fairly standard you'll be able to get parts pretty much anywhere in the world. Wherever there are vehicles, there are spare parts suppliers and mechanics who will help you. Here are a few things I carry:

- **Spare fuses.** An assortment of blade fuses for the van's electrical system and also spare fuses for the electrical system in the living space.
- **Box of random bits and pieces:** screws, random fittings, Gaffa tape, bits of wire, cable ties and other things that can sometimes come in handy.
- **Spare engine oil.** I had difficulty finding my oil in other countries so I carry a couple of litres spare – I

have a small leak so I carry this incase it gets worse.

- **Spare differential oil.** I only carry this because my rear differential has a slight leak and I have to top it up every few hundred miles. Although I fixed it last week so I'll ditch it now.
- **Radiator hose repair tape.** For temporary repairs in case a hose fails – and they do fail.

Other equipment and bits that may be useful

- **Torches.** LED Maglite and also an LED head torch. The head torch gets used the most – especially cooking outside, or for fixing the van.
- **Jerry can of extra fuel.** This could be worth carrying if you're going to be well away from civilisation for some time. Or for peace of mind in case you ever accidentally run out of fuel. But I don't bother.
- **Electric hook up cable.** If I'm ever near a power outlet I can plug this in to power my electrical system and charge my batteries. I don't stay on campsites so I rarely use this, but it's good to have as a backup.
- **Rope and straps.** Useful for securing things on the roof.

Documents

I have an A4 folder to keep all my important documents together, kept behind the driver's seat. It makes me look organised when the police stop me and ask to see my documents – they see the organised folder and suddenly no longer care. Here are the documents I carry:

- **Van insurance certificate.** I printed this myself because it was issued electronically as a pdf – most insurance certificates are now electronic. This is enough to provide proof of insurance in the UK and the EU. A 'green card' is not necessary (it used to be something that you had to carry if you were travelling out of the UK) and most insurers don't issue these anymore.

- **The latest MOT certificate.** No one has ever asked to see this but I carry it anyway.
- **Vehicle registration document.** This is the V5 document in the UK. It's important to carry this at all times as proof that you are the owner of your van.
- **Driving licence.**
- **Passport.**

It's a good idea to make a digital scan or photograph of the important documents in case they get lost. For example, passport, driving licence and van documents. I use the Evernote app for this, as I mentioned earlier.

Things to carry in the van by law for Europe

If you are driving in Europe you are required by law to carry certain items with you in your vehicle. This varies slightly from country to country so I just carry everything (it doesn't take up much space) so I know I'm covered whatever EU country I'm in:

- **Two warning triangles and reflective vests**
- **Breathalysers**
- **Spare bulbs**
- **Headlamp adaptors:** for driving on the other side of the road
- **First aid kit**
- **GB sticker** – I prefer the small ones that stick on the number plates

Go for a test run

Before venturing out into the world with your van, you might find it useful to go on a practice camping trip in your home country first. It'll give you a good idea of any things you might have forgotten or overlooked. But also, you might realise that you don't use many of the things you thought you would, so you can go back for round two of shedding your possessions.

I didn't do a test run or a practice camping trip. The first time I drove the van it was to get a ferry out of the UK. But a test run could have made things a bit easier.

Panic packing

When going into the 'unknown' it can be tempting to bring loads of unnecessary stuff, justifying it with a 'just in case' mindset. But it'll probably never get used. Remember, other countries usually have all the shops, parts and difficult to get things that your country has.

What if you bring too much stuff?

If at any point in your journey you realise you've got too much stuff you can either give it away, sell it or post it to friends or family who can store it for you.

Storage in a van

Losing things in the van is really annoying and you have to turn the whole van upside-down. It happened a lot in the beginning. But as time has gone on, I've become more organised and efficient with the storage and everything tends to find its best place. Here's how (and where) I store things in my van:

- **Food.** I have a few different areas to store food and I'll go through it in the 'Cooking & eating' chapter. But generally it's categorised into: fresh things, dry things, tins, spices, condiments and miscellaneous.
- **Kitchen utensils.** I keep a saucepan and frying pan on the inside of the kitchen cupboard doors using hooks. Commonly used cooking utensils are hung on the wall above the kitchen unit and all other utensils

are in the kitchen drawer.

- **Clothes.** I keep most of my clothes in the storage space above the cab. It's out of the way but still easily accessible.
- **Tools.** I keep most of them under the sofa-bed in a toolbox with a few commonly used tools (screwdriver, adjustable spanner, etc.) in the chest of drawers for easy access.
- **Spare parts and bits.** I have a plastic box full of random bits and spare parts – clips, screws, fuses, wire, etc. This is also under the sofa-bed next to the toolbox.
- **Guest storage.** I have spare storage space above the cab that will fit large backpacks. There's also some space at the back of the van (under the desk) for more big bags or suitcases.
- **Frequently used things.** Electronics, cables, chargers, random bits and pieces that I use from day to day I keep in the chest of drawers. I made wooden separators in each drawer to make things easier to find – search the blog for 'van upgrades' to have a look.
- **Infrequently used things.** I use another plastic storage box under the sofa bed for random things I hardly ever use. When this box starts overflowing, that's when I get rid of stuff.
- **Bike and large items.** I have a strong galvanised mesh roof rack which is really useful. As well as the solar panels being mounted there I also store my bike, a couple of fold up chairs, a folding table, hosepipe and electric hookup cable. And when it's a clear night it's a good place to lay and star gaze.
- **Overflow.** When there's a few people living out of the van, the shower room and the front seats often gets used to store things like bags, guitars or whatever.

Get to know your van

I think it's worth spending time to familiarise yourself with some of the workings of your van. Just a little bit of knowledge about engines and mechanics can help you a lot when you have problems. And at the very least it will give you enough understanding so you can discuss the problem with a mechanic.

I agree that if you take a look under the bonnet of your van, it looks complicated. All those tubes and wires and lumps of metal. But if you look at anything from this overview perspective it's confusing and difficult to understand. Once you have an idea of how an engine works, and once you know the basic functions of the main parts, the overall picture (all the stuff under the bonnet) becomes a lot easier to understand.

You can learn a lot by doing small jobs yourself on your van. It could be turning a nut to adjust the handbrake cable, changing a battery or replacing the fan belt. YouTube is a great resource to help you do these things – it's how I've learnt pretty much everything I know about engines. All these little lessons will add up over time and eventually you'll get to know and understand the whole engine.

After spending five months working on my van, and doing all these little jobs myself, I had a good idea where everything was in the engine bay and underneath my van. I became familiar with everything – how things looked, sounded and smelled. This familiarity gave me the knowledge and confidence to be able to fix it myself when I had problems on the road.

Here are some things you can do to get more familiar with your van's engine:

- **Try to do any simple jobs yourself.** Like replacing pumps, belts, brakes, valves, sensors, hoses, etc. Rather than getting a mechanic to do it. There's a guy on YouTube called 'ChrisFix'. He shows you how to do just about any job on your vehicle. I've learnt a lot from this guy.
- **Get the manual/documentation for your engine.** This will have everything you'll ever need to know about your engine: how to dismantle it, service it and fix it. Keep this in your van. I have all the service manuals for my van on my computer. I'd be stuck without them.
- **Look under the bonnet.** Familiarise yourself with where things are located, referring to the manual as you go.
- **Don't be scared of doing things yourself.** Vehicles are designed to be serviced, repaired and worked on. You are allowed to do this yourself.
- **Go on test runs.** Drive your van around in the weeks before setting off on your travels. Observe everything about it and get to know how it runs. It's better that it breaks now, in your home country, rather than in the Atlas Mountains.

Of course, you don't have to learn about mechanics or do any of this stuff. It's not an absolute requirement but if you plan on doing a lot of travelling, it helps. If you have the money you can get breakdown cover and leave it for someone else to fix. That's also fine. In an ideal world you'd know a bit about your engine as well as having breakdown cover. But at the very least you should know:

- How to check the engine oil level and top it up
- How to check the coolant level and top it up
- How to change a wheel

It might also be good to know about some of the common

fault conditions of an engine and how to diagnose simple problems. I'll talk about this later in the 'Van maintenance & problems' chapter.

Fix van-specific faults

All vans have their own specific quirks, faults and known problems. These things are useful to know about before you set off and before they become a bigger problem. I Googled things like 'LDV Convoy problem' and 'LDV Convoy help'. I found message boards with people asking for help with their broken LDVs which gave me an idea of some of the common problems with my van. Those were the problems I investigated or fixed, before they happened to me. Or you can just ask a good mechanic to do this – preferably a mechanic who specialises in vans and commercial vehicles.

Here's an example: A known problem with my van is that the dual mass flywheel fails after about 100k miles. It's pretty much sure to happen and eventually it will damage the starter motor and cause the engine to not start. So I had the flywheel replaced with a different one (a standard single flywheel that does not have this problem) before I set off. Now I don't need to worry about it.

Another common problem on my van is that the immobiliser can fail, causing the engine to not start. I prepared for this by making sure I'd be able to start the van by bypassing the immobiliser with a bit of wire (using the electrical diagrams to help me). It's things like this that I'd rather work out before I set off so I know what to do if it happens when I'm on the road.

Things to check on your van before you set off

Here are some jobs and checks you should do on your van before setting off. If you're not comfortable doing any of this you can take it to a mechanic, explaining that you're going away for some time and you'd like to have any potential problems fixed. Or you can look up how to do it on YouTube (my favourite). For example, you might search for 'how to check brakes'.

- **Brakes.** If you only have a few hundred miles of break pads left you might want to change these before you set off.
- **Coolant.** Check there is enough coolant (between minimum and maximum markers on the coolant overflow tank) and that there are no leaks. As for the mixture, a 50% mix is usually a safe bet for most engines and suitable for most climates.
- **Oil.** Change the oil and make sure the level is between the minimum and maximum markers on the dip stick. Too much oil will damage the engine, as will too little. Get good quality oil and make sure it is the right specification for your engine – refer to the van's manual.
- **Tyres.** Check for any damage, tears, bulges or leaks. If there's only a few hundred miles left on the tyres, you might as well change them before you go. Also, certain countries require by law that you have winter tyres, so it's worth checking this.
- **Change filters.** The oil filter should be changed when you change the oil, and there's no harm replacing the air filter either.
- **Fan belt.** If your belt is squeaking, makes any unusual noises or has cracks in it, it should be replaced. They are cheap and it's a straightforward job. It's better to replace it now than have it failing when you're out on the road.
- **Check/replace timing belt.** If this belt fails it will wreck a lot of other bits in the engine and it's a lot of work to fix. The timing belt should be replaced as a precautionary measure at intervals suggested by the van manufacturer. Some engines have a chain

instead of a belt, which last a lot longer and may never need replacing.

- **Leaks.** It's quite normal for old engines to have slight leaks in various places and often it's not much to worry about. The important thing is to keep an eye on it in case it gets worse. If you have to keep topping up a fluid on a regular basis, get it fixed. Otherwise, just keep an eye on it.

- **Rubber hoses.** Visually inspect rubber hoses and wire looms for damage. Hoses and insulated wires can get damaged over time from rubbing against metal edges or on other components in the engine bay. So make sure nothing is chafing because eventually it will wear right through and cause damage.

- **Pay attention to odd sounds, smells or warning lights.** Know how everything should be when your engine is running well, so when something goes wrong you'll know about it.

Insurance, documents and legal stuff

These things are going to vary with every country. Being from the UK, I'll share what I have to do.

MOT

This is the annual road-worthiness test for vehicles in the UK. As far as I know, if you have a UK registered van, the UK is the only place you can get the MOT test done. So it means you have to make a visit to the UK every year. Although, I did (accidentally) spend 18 months out of the UK and nothing flagged up when I came back.

If you ever find yourself far away from the UK with your MOT expired, you could always ask a local garage to take your van through whatever the road safety test is in the country you're in. This is by no means a solution. But if for some reason you get questioned by police without an MOT, you'll have an easier time. I'm not saying this is legal (it's probably complicated), I'm just saying it's all you can do if you're in this situation and at least you'll know your van is safe to drive. I'll clarify: I'm not recommending you do this and it will probably invalidate your insurance.

Tax

In the UK we pay vehicle tax. It goes towards making new roads and fixing the potholes in old ones. But you still have to pay it even if you're not spending any time in the UK, otherwise insurance will be invalid. Vehicle tax is now all electronic, which makes things a lot easier. You buy it online and you no longer have to display a tax disk in your windscreen.

Reclassify as a camper van

If your van is self-converted, you should update the vehicle type on the V5 document, if it hasn't been already. This is a legal requirement (although I've never heard of it being enforced) and some motorhome insurers will not cover you if the van doesn't have this official classification. This process can take a couple of weeks so it's best to do it now before you set off. You have to send the original copy of the vehicle document (the V5) off to the DVLA and wait for it to be returned – it's all done by post.

For more information on how to reclassify your van, see vandogtraveller.com/reclassify-camper. It's a straight forward process but you have to make sure to follow the instructions exactly as they say, giving clear photographic evidence for each of their requirements.

Have a postal address

Many things like insurance renewal, bank statements, tax and travel bookings can now all be done electronically. But we still need an address to be able to use these services, and to own a vehicle. I use my parent's address. For all the services I use, I choose to receive all communication (like bank statements) by email. For me, there's nothing really important that should come through the post.

But if you do need to receive post, as a traveller with no fixed address, there are many services that can help you. These are usually called mail forwarding or mail scanning services. You pay a monthly fee and have all your post sent to them. You'll get notified by email when you have post and you're able to see a scan of the outside of the letter in your online account. From here you decide if you want the contents scanned, the letter discarded (or shredded) or have it forwarded to you.

Van insurance

There are two ways to go about this. One way is to just get standard van insurance and the other way is to get motorhome insurance. Proper motorhome insurance is the best bet, since it offers better cover for contents and personal possessions. But in the UK you can only usually take these policies out if the van is officially registered as a motor-caravan. Some insurers may consider a vehicle that is not registered as a motor-caravan on a case by case basis – I've read this on a couple of insurers' websites, but what they take into consideration, I don't know.

If your van is in the process of being converted, most insurers will give you a minimum of three months for the work to be complete. After this time they will request evidence of the conversion – a copy of the updated V5 document and possibly a few photographs.

Insurance cover in other EU countries (outside the UK)

Many motorhome insurance policies can provide full cover in Europe (outside of the UK) for the year. By default, most insurers will advertise as giving you full cover out of England for 90 days.

But it's worth knowing that every insurance policy taken out in the UK has to, by law, provide minimum cover required in every EU country for the duration of the policy. This is from the first point on the EU motor insurance directive: 'obliges all motor vehicles in the EU to be covered by compulsory third party insurance (all passengers are covered, throughout the EU).'

Insurance companies don't tell you this though, and they may even deny it if you ask them, but they have no choice. OK, minimal cover is not exactly ideal, but at least you know you are legal when this 90 days runs out.

You can read this insurance directive here: vandogtraveller.com/eu-insurance-directive.

Also, I've made a list of some of the popular UK motorhome insurers here: vandogtraveller.com/motorhome-insurance.

Insurance in non-EU countries
If you're travelling through a non-EU country you'll have to either arrange for extra cover from your current insurer (although many UK insurers will probably not offer this) or buy insurance at the border of the country.

Buying insurance at the border is fairly quick and easy. They just need your vehicle registration form and a few details from you. Depending on the country you'll either get a reassuring certificate with a hologram, or just a little bit of paper with some guy's signature scribbled on it.

This kind of insurance (bought at country borders) is much cheaper if your van is officially classified as a motorhome, rather than a normal van that could be used for business or commercial purposes. Make sure you tell them your van is for leisure use and not for business.

Health and travel insurance

If you are an EU citizen you get a national insurance card for emergency medical treatment. This means if you need medical treatment anywhere in the EU you just pay a little bit of money instead of thousands. But now the UK is leaving the EU I don't know if we'll still have any agreements like this. I guess we'll have to get out separate medical insurance. I don't know. I'll update this book when the time comes.

You might want to take out extra health and travel insurance, especially if you're doing any dangerous sports. There are now loads of companies offering all different levels of travel insurance. The best thing is to look at comparison sites where you can easily compare many insurance policies at a glance.

Breakdown cover

The thought of breaking down in the middle of nowhere can be a bit worrying. Breakdown recovery can ease that worry and give you peace of mind. But I've never had breakdown cover. It was always out of the question because of the cost. You can expect to pay over £200 a year for cover in the EU from companies like The AA or RAC. And they may not cover you if your van is over a certain age or weight.

But there are some alternatives. Many people travelling Europe by van have had a good experience with the German insurance company, ADAC, who offer breakdown cover for the whole of Europe. They'll accept pretty much any vehicle regardless of weight or size, and their prices are good. For more information see their website adac.de. Many of their operators speak English, if not just ask.

Another option is to get breakdown cover when you buy your van insurance. I've found that most motorhome insurers offer EU breakdown cover as a policy add-on at a fair price. I was recently quoted £90 for a year of European cover with no restrictions on the vehicle's age. For some reason I didn't take it. So I still don't have breakdown cover.

Cut your ties

Over the years we sign up to all sorts of services and contracts that take direct debits from our bank each month. Now is a good time to cancel anything you don't really need – especially if you're leaving the country. The mobile phone contract is probably the most difficult to get out of. Most phone contracts in the UK are now a minimum of two years and it's usually not cost effective to use it in other countries. There are a few options:

- **Amend the contract.** Call your provider and explain you want to travel. Maybe they can offer some kind of roaming deal that makes it worth keeping your contact. This will become more likely in the next few years as operators scrap roaming fees.
- **Pause the contract.** Providers usually allow a maximum of six months to pause your contract. During this time you don't pay anything but after the pause time has elapsed the contact resumes as normal. Depending on how far you are into your contract you may be able to extend this six months.
- **Cancel the contract.** This is possible and there's a lot of advice online about doing this, but it's always considered on a case by case basis. You'd have to write a good letter, something along the lines of your life situation unexpectedly changing, and that you're moving to another country.

With things like this, I've found that rules can always be

bent. Sometimes you have to persist and not take no for an answer. If one operator cannot help you, hang up and speak to another – it's amazing how much their helpfulness can vary.

Access your money

It can cost a lot to use your normal bank card in other countries – the transaction fees and lower than average exchange rates will soon add up. You need to have a card that can be used everywhere you intend on travelling, and that gives you a good exchange rate with minimal transaction fees. Here are a couple of options:

- **A Credit card.** They often have good exchange rates and low transaction fees when used in other countries. At the time of writing (2017), the Halifax Clarity card (in the UK) looks like one of the best options to use whilst travelling – it has good exchange rates and zero transaction fees. The other advantage of a credit card is that it gives you a high level of protection if your account is used fraudulently or if a purchase goes wrong in some way.
- **A Cash travel card.** There are several companies offering cash cards that can be topped up with a currency of your choice and used for free in most retailers and ATMs around the world. I use a Caxton FX travel card (Mastercard) for everything – withdrawing money, buying diesel and shopping. I can top it up using an app on my phone as well as check my balance and transactions.

It's also useful to make a habit of carrying a bit of cash with you in your van. I once filled the van full with diesel in a remote part of Greece only to find they didn't take card – there are many fuel stations that don't. I didn't have any cash so I wrote him an 'I owe you' and took his bank details. I paid him via a bank transfer when I got to Athens. But it would have been easier if I had cash.

Set a date

I spent the whole winter working outside on the van for ten hours every day. It seemed to never end. I'd fix one problem and another appeared. I really wanted this to work and I'd become obsessed. I hardly showered and I grew my first beard. I was sick of working on the van and I just couldn't see a time when I'd be totally ready to go.

So I set a date. There were still some things left to do but I decided I could do them when I was on the road. I booked a ferry from Dover (UK) to Dunkirk (France). Now I had to leave on that day no matter what. Time for the countdown. But I didn't tell anyone until just a few days before – I didn't quite believe this was actually going to happen.

Setting a date is when things start to become real. Without setting a date, plans slide. I could have easily spent a lot longer working on my van but I had to draw the line somewhere. This forced me to give priority to only the most important things. The rest I could do once I'd set off, whilst I was on the road.

Based on my experience, this would be my advice: Be careful of waiting to feel completely ready, because it may never come. Sometimes you just have to take the leap. As long as you have the essentials you'll be fine. Just go. All the other things you can sort out along the way. It may not feel comfortable and it may feel like things are working against you, but it'll all fall into place.

6

Make a run for it

There's only so much preparation you can do. If you've done the things in the last chapter, you're pretty much ready to go. It's time to travel and make it all happen.

For me this was the most scary and exciting part of it all. I felt like there were so many things that could go wrong and all the worst case scenarios were running around my head. I wasn't even sure the van would make it 200 miles to the ferry port without breaking down. A few weeks before this the engine wasn't running.

A friend gave me this advice: For everything you can't control, forget it. There's no point worrying. If problems come up, solutions will also come up. Just deal with it at the time.

I was still making last minute adjustments to the van the day I left. I packed a bag of clothes and a box of food minutes before I set off for the ferry port. I'm disorganised.

With friends (including animals) or alone?

My plan was to set off alone but I'm glad I didn't. I'd only just learnt to drive a car and now I was about to drive a big van on the other side of the road in a country I didn't know – and live in it as my full time home. I didn't feel like I knew what I was doing, and I didn't.

But I was lucky to have two friends who I set off with. Friends can help you laugh when things go wrong – like when you forget what side of the road to drive on – or when you have to reverse all the way back down a one-way road whilst everyone beeps their horns and swears at you. My friends stayed for a few weeks and we adjusted to this new life together, except that they had to go back to their normal lives and I would continue my journey. When they left I felt comfortable and ready to explore Europe on my own.

After I'd dropped my friends off at the airport I was completely alone in the Swiss Alps and that's when the real adventure started. I had this crazy overwhelming feeling: every decision was down to me. No one to discuss routes with. No help pulling out onto big roads. At first, it was scary. But I knew what this was. It was the feeling of complete and utter freedom.

I like being with people and friends, but being alone is quite a different experience. Completely different things happen when you're alone. It's much more personal. Travelling alone has taught me a lot. I like to have a few months alone and then a few months with people, alternating like this – it just seems to happen naturally.

Choose travel company wisely

I met a guy in Morocco who made a camper-bike (a metal box with a bed inside and solar panel on top, welded onto a motorbike that was chopped in half). He travelled North Africa with his girlfriend for six months. They broke up after that. He was saying how living in such a small space with someone is the ultimate test of a relationship. I agree. Although, his space was very small – about 1m x 2m x 1m.

If you're going to be living with someone in such a small space it's important they tick a few of these boxes:

- **Are they happy?** Travelling with a negative person will drag you down and change the whole experience. They might be a good friend in normal life but for travelling with it might be different.
- **Do you get on with each other?** It's important to be able to laugh, having a similar sense of humour and outlook on life.
- **Do your lifestyles suit each other?** Maybe you like to get up before sunrise and your friend likes to sleep in until 11am. It can makes things difficult in a van – although, it depends on your setup. With things like this you'll have to be willing to compromise with each other.
- **Do your styles of travelling suit each other?** An obsessive planner might not work with a fully free-spirited spontaneous kind of traveller. I'm not saying that's always the case – sometimes it can balance out.

As for dogs. They make great friends to travel with. They're happy doing whatever as long as they're with their pack (you). They're also warm. Loads of people travel with dogs and it's totally possible. All the travelling dogs I've met seem to love it.

Cats as well. I met a couple who travelled in their camper with their cat. They would camp for a few weeks at a time in the countryside. I was impressed at how the cat would always come back to the van. I guess there was no one else around to feed it.

Chickens as well. I met a family with chickens in their van. The chickens roamed free outside when they were camped up. At the back of the van they had a chicken coup and the chickens would go back inside at sunset. Eggs for breakfast.

For cats and dogs you need to make sure you have all the vaccinations and pet passports if travelling to different countries. If your dog has not had its latest vaccinations they might have to put it in quarantine for a set period of time, which can be expensive. So make sure you research the country you're going to first and what paperwork is required for you to bring animals.

To plan a route?

Some people might want to plan an exact route before setting off, knowing exact stop off points of where to stay and where to have breaks. Other people might want to just make it up as they go along. And then there's everything in between. Whatever works for you.

My plan has always been simple: go south for winter and north for summer whilst having a good time on the way. I think it's fine to not know exactly where you're going. The best adventures start this way.

Don't get me wrong, a plan has its place but often it's just a starting point. A plan can make you feel more comfortable in the beginning as you get used to this way of living and travelling. But as time goes on you might find you get into the flow and the plan becomes less relevant.

Some people have emailed me saying they're going to follow my route. But that's not really why I put it on my blog. The beauty of travel is that you do it in your way, taking your own route, following your own signs and clues from the things that interest you. The route you take is a personal thing. It's your journey.

However you decide to do it, you'll need a map.

Navigation

I use a Garmin Nuvi 50 GPS. It's one of the more basic Garmin models but it has more than enough features for me and it's always worked without problems for the past two years. I've used a couple of cheap unbranded GPS units in the past (eBay) but they've never lasted more than a few months.

As well as my GPS I use Google maps on my phone when looking for places to stay – I'll explain this in the chapter, 'Freecamping & where to stay'.

Of course, the old fashioned paper map still works fine. I met a girl travelling Europe in her van using torn bits of an old paper map. She seemed to manage. I've also met people travelling with no map at all. But I prefer a GPS. Here's why:

- **Maps are easily updated.** New roads are constantly being built and changed but with a GPS you always have an up-to-date map. Just connect the GPS to the computer and click 'update' using the software that comes with it.

- **Easier and safer.** If you're driving in a foreign country you already have enough to think about.
- **Store POI (points of interest).** You can load lists of whatever you want on to a GPS: camping spots, fuel stations, etc. You can even create your own POI lists and share them with others. There are some on my blog you can download for free which include lists of freecamping spots, services, all the Lidl supermarkets in Europe and other things: vandogtraveller.com/europe-poi-gpx.
- **Track your route.** I use my GPS to record my track. Every few hundred miles I plug the GPS into my laptop and upload the track data using the Garmin Basecamp software. In Basecamp I can mark all the places I stopped with an icon (I use a little Anchor icon) and add a few notes. That's how I make the map on my blog that shows my track and all the places I've stayed. See the map here: vandogtraveller.com/track.
- **Speed limit warnings.** Depending on the device you can set it to give a visual or audio alert if you go over the speed limit. This is really useful.
- **Route preferences.** You can calculate your route to avoid toll roads, take the slow scenic route or take a fast route. Also very useful.

I prefer to mute the voice on my GPS because it's not so helpful and I want to listen to music when driving. I also prefer the symbol of a bird rather than a car, so I changed that too.

Getting different maps

When I went to Morocco, I had to update my Garmin with a map of Morocco. But rather than buy the official (and expensive) map from Garmin I found a website offering open source maps for a much more reasonable price. I paid £10 and used instructions provided to load it on to my GPS. It works great. There are maps for pretty much every device and for every country. The website is: gpstravelmaps.com.

Or use your smartphone GPS

You can also use an app on your smartphone instead of a dedicated GPS device. There's now a huge choice of navigation apps but it's worth getting one that works fully offline so it doesn't use up your mobile data – and because you might not always have internet. If you decide to use your phone as GPS you'll need to get a mount to hold your phone in a good position whilst driving. You'll also need a phone power cable that plugs into the van's cigarette lighter socket.

Last minute hesitation

You're about to make it all happen. This is where the fears and anxieties can start to creep in again. It's totally normal. If you keep hesitating, or if you need a bit of a push, skip to the chapter, 'Fears, excuses & actually doing it' near the end of the book.

It'll all be fine. Let's goooooo.

Escape the island (ferry routes out of the UK)

Once you're in mainland Europe you can get nearly everywhere by land. Even China. So if you're based in the UK and want to explore other countries, this bit is for you.

The cheapest and most frequent routes operate from the south of England to the north of France. When I first set off I got a ferry from Dover (UK) to Dunkirk (France) costing £50 – just £16 each between me and my two friends.

There are also several ferry routes from the UK that land you in a good place for exploring the north of Europe and the Scandinavian countries. The Hull to Rotterdam ferry is one of them, but they operate less frequently and cost a lot more.

If you want to go as far south as possible in a short amount of time, there are two main ferry routes from the south of England (Portsmouth or Plymouth) to the north of Spain (Santander or Bilbao). I used the Plymouth to Santander ferry when I was going to Morocco for the winter after spending autumn in the UK. It costs a lot more than the ferry to France but it saves a lot of driving and actually works out cheaper if you include the diesel and toll road costs in France.

When looking at ferry prices and booking, I use a comparison site like AFerry.com or DirectFerry.com. Or you can just turn up at the ferry port and buy a ticket there – sometimes it's cheaper and sometimes not. Here are some things that affect the cost of the ferry:

- **The size of your van.** The wider and higher your van, the more expensive the ferry will be. My van is 5.4m in length but I'd choose the 5m option when booking online – it's in multiples of 1m. I'd also do the same with the height and round it down to the nearest option. The price can differ quite a lot by doing this. As long as your van looks like it roughly matches the numbers on your booking, it should be fine.
- **The classification of your van.** Some ferry companies charge less for a motorhome, as opposed to a commercial van. So if it's an option, make sure you select 'motorhome' or 'camper' when booking.
- **Time.** If you're booking online - the earlier you book, the cheaper it will be.
- **Discount codes.** It's always worth Googling for discount codes and current offers before booking online. For example, I might search for 'AFerry discount code 2017' and use that code when ordering online.

- **Accommodation and food.** I prefer not to have a cabin if possible. On an overnight ferry (like Plymouth to Santander which takes 24 hours) I bring a blanket, food and water and set up my own camp in a quiet corner. It saves £70 or so.
- **Number of passengers.** It usually doesn't cost much more (sometimes nothing) to add another person to your ferry crossing with a van. So if there's more than just you travelling on the ferry then you can save a lot by splitting the cost between you.

Getting the ferry to Morocco

If you're in Europe and you want to get to Morocco with your van (I highly recommend it), this bit is for you.

Morocco is just a few miles away from Spain and easily accessed by ferry. But since Morocco is out of the EU, travelling here is a little different. I don't recommend doing what I normally do and work everything out as you go along. It's a bit more confusing in Morocco. Suddenly there are no orderly queues. And in the words of a policeman, peering through my open window, 'this isn't Europe anymore'.

There are four things you need to do to get to Morocco with your van. The following steps are based on my experience travelling from Algeciras (Spain) to Tangier Med (Morocco) in 2016.

1. Get a ticket. Ferries are so frequent that there's no need to buy a ticket in advance. It's easier and cheaper to buy a ticket directly at the ferry port. On the way to the port there were many people by the road side trying to flag me down to sell me a ferry ticket. These people are genuine but it's cheaper buying directly at the port. So head straight for the ferry port and park in the carpark. I got an open return for €150. Half an hour later I was on a ferry to Africa.

2. Immigration. When you board the ferry you get given a form to fill in. This is for immigration. You fill this in and return it to a guy sat at a table in the cafeteria. He may ask you further questions about why you're visiting Morocco and where exactly you intend to visit. Say you'll be staying in campsites. It's much easier.

3. Import vehicle. After getting off the ferry in Morocco all cars are checked by customs. Whilst waiting here you have to get out your van and pick up a vehicle import form from one of the customs offices. Eventually an officer will come to the van and ask to see the completed form along with your vehicle registration document (V5 in the UK). This wasn't obvious to me. The whole thing was a bit hectic and it took me a while to work out what to do – and none of the officers spoke English.

At this point they may want to check inside the van. Some people were having to unpack their whole cars and even their bags. But as soon as I opened the side door of my van, he no longer seemed to care.

Side note: whilst waiting for an official to come and check your papers, some local Moroccans will go round the cars selling stuff. I bought a SIM card for €3 and topped it up with 4GB of data for €5. That was useful.

4. Vehicle Insurance (skip if you're already insured). Just down the road (about 100m) from customs there's an office that says 'assurance automobile' with a carpark next to it. This is where you need to go with your vehicle registration and import document to buy vehicle insurance if you are not already covered for Morocco – most standard EU insurance doesn't cover you.

Problems with insurance and vehicle classification

At this time my van was still registered as a 'panel van' which meant insurance was going to cost a lot more – €450 for three months in Morocco. The guy insisted (luckily he spoke a bit of English) that he can only go by what the registration paper says. I offered him a tour inside my van to prove that it is a camper and I'm not using it for business reasons, but I couldn't persuade him. He wrote down 450 in big numbers and slid the paper across the desk to me.

So I went back to the customs office (step three) and got a customs official to write 'caravan' on my vehicle import paper. I took it back to the insurance office and the problem was solved. The insurance price went down from €450 to €180 (after convincing him that I didn't write 'caravan' myself). Still expensive but it's a big difference. That was my first lesson in Morocco: never take no for a final answer.

Refilling with gas (LPG)

I mentioned earlier that refillable gas bottles are the most convenient and cheapest way to store gas in your van, as opposed to the bottles that you exchange. I'll talk a bit about that now, as well as how to fill up with water.

There's some uncertainty (mainly on the internet) about whether or not you're able to fill refillable LPG bottles at fuel stations. The LPG pumps at fuel stations are intended to be used to fill cars that run on LPG, so it can raise concern amongst staff when they see you filling a bottle directly. If you do get questioned about it, just explain that the bottle is designed to be filled like this (which it is) and that it has an automatic cut-off valve making it impossible to overfill – it shuts off at 80%.

So whether it is illegal or not to fill a bottle directly, I have no idea. All that matters to me is if it's safe or not, and it is. In all the countries I've been to in Europe (including the UK), I've never had a problem directly filling my bottle at fuel stations. If staff question what you're doing, which they sometimes do, just confidently say it's no problem and it's a special gas bottle. That's always done the trick for me.

LPG filler adapters

Different countries use different nozzle designs (there are four that I know of) so you'll have to carry some adapters to make sure you can always refill with gas. These are the LPG filler connectors/adapters I carry in my van:

1. Bayonet connector
2. ACME connector
3. Dish connector
4. Euro connector (or Euro nozzle)

The Euro connector is starting to become the standard due to it being a more safe and robust design. Eventually, the other connectors will get phased out but it'll probably take a long time – that goes for Europe and the US. For more information on what countries use what connectors, have a look here: mylpg.eu/adapters/.

How to fill your gas bottle

I had no idea how to use the LPG gas pumps at first – it's not exactly like filling up with diesel. Instructions are usually given on the LPG pump but it can still take a bit of practice. If you're not sure how to fill the bottle yourself the first time, you can just ask for one of the staff to help you. But it goes something like this:

1. Work out which adapter you need by looking at the pump nozzle. Screw the required adapter onto your bottle filler and make sure it's tight – when I got my bottle, the adapter was loosely screwed on and gas went everywhere.
2. Mate the pump nozzle to your bottle's filler inlet. You

have to pull the trigger to lock it into place – each type of connector requires a slightly different knack. Once the nozzle is locked in place you don't have to hold it.

3. Press the push button (usually coloured green) on the pump and wait for it to fill. The pump will automatically stop when the bottle hits the 80% limit.

4. Squeeze the trigger to remove the nozzle. There might be some compressed gas that will escape as you remove it, and it can make a sudden 'pshh' sound. I usually turn my head away when I do this.

Where to get LPG

Every country I've been to in Europe, LPG has been widely available. But not every fuel station has LPG, it's just a select few. To see which ones have it, have a look at lpgstations.com.

How long does gas last?

It depends on how many gas appliances you run in your van and how often you use them. And some things like heaters will use a lot more gas than the kitchen gas hob. In the summer my 11kg gas cylinder will last at least three months before I have to refill it – that's for daily cooking and tea making. But in winter, I'd expect it to last about six weeks. My bottle costs around €10 to fill up – it's about 17L of gas.

Filling up with water

I have an on-board 70L fresh water tank that I use for my main water supply – washing, cooking and sometimes drinking. Refilling the tank with water just becomes one of those weekly tasks you have to do. In Europe most of the mains water is safe to drink but if it tastes or smells a bit strange I'd drink bottled water. I've only been ill once because I drank bad water – but it did smell stagnant and I shouldn't have drank it.

Finding water

Ease of being able to get water differs between countries – hotter countries tend to have more taps dotted about. But in all the countries I've been to I've never not been able to fill up with water. It's everywhere. Here are some places to get water from:

- **Fuel stations.** Many fuel stations have a tap somewhere on the forecourt. Sometimes they are a bit hidden out of view so what I do is park the van and walk around or ask one of the staff if there is a tap. This is the main way I get water and I've never had a problem. If they don't have water, I go to the next fuel station.
- **Campsites.** Some campsites will be happy to give you water and some won't, even if you offer a couple of Euros – I guess they are trying to run a camping business. But if there's one nearby, it's worth asking. This was how I used to fill up before I discovered the taps in fuel stations.
- **Car wash.** The self service car washes often have tap on the inside of the wash building. If it's a hand-wash place, just ask one of the staff if you can fill your tank.
- **Utility taps.** These are small manhole covers in the ground with access to a tap inside by lifting the hinged cover. They are used mainly in urban areas by local councils for watering the grass and flowers – healthy green grass or a flower bed is a good clue. These are usually just to the side of the main pavement or on the grass verge. This could be classed as stealing. I'm not sure.
- **Motorhome services.** There are many free motorhome service stops throughout Europe. It's usually an area where you can get water and empty your toilet and grey waste. Some are free and others

you might have to pay.

- **Village water well or communal tap.** Many villages have a communal well or water source. Some might still be with a hand pump and some might have been converted to have a normal tap. In Morocco they have wells with a pulley and a bucket. The only problem is that it can be difficult to get the water from the bucket into the van's tank.
- **Using an app.** My friend cycles long distances on her bike. She uses a map on her phone that shows locations of water points where she can fill up. Some are not accessible by van but many are. The app is called Maps.me.

Getting water into the van

This will depend on your van conversion and how your water is stored. My tank is filled via a water fill point mounted on the back of my kitchen unit, and is accessed by opening the side door.

I use a five metre length of garden hose (kept coiled up on the van's roof) with a garden hose connector that can fit onto threaded outdoor taps. I carry three different screw connector sizes which cover all the taps I've come across in Europe: 1/2", 3/4" and 1". Sometimes a tap might not be threaded, in which case I just force the rubber hose over the tap spout, which makes a good enough seal for the purpose of filling my tank.

In the US, garden hose connectors have slightly different sized threads. The best thing to do is to go into a garden or home store and get the most common threaded connectors to fit outdoor taps.

Sometimes you might find a tap with the handle missing. It's usually because the owner doesn't want anyone to use it and so it's best to look somewhere else, if possible. But if you really need water you can use a pair of pliers to open and close it, or carry a spare tap handle with you in the van. I'm not suggesting you steal water. I'm just saying, if you're desperate.

Sometimes it's not possible to get the van close enough to the tap, or maybe the length of hose isn't long enough. In this case you can fill plastic water containers to carry the water to your van. Either use a funnel to pour the water into your tank or syphon it in using a length of hose, holding the container of water up high – or put it on the roof. Collapsable water containers (the ones that can pack down flat) can be good things to have for this. But as I say, I've found fuel stations to be the best and most convenient way to get water.

Carrying more water

If you're spending a long time away from civilisation (and water) you can carry extra water in extra plastic containers. You can get large 25L water containers in camping shops that can be stored inside the van or on the roof. I have a huge galvanised roof rack that lets me store tonnes of stuff, including extra water if I want. But I've never found it to be necessary – I'd rather use the space for my bike and herb garden.

How long will it last?

Water gets used quickly. My tank is 70L and this lasts me seven days of normal van use – which is still nothing like normal usage in a house. I can make it last two weeks if I need to but this took me a bit of practice.

When I set off with my two friends we'd have competitions to see who could use the least water for showering and washing hair. The winner was 1.7L. We used a pen to mark the level on the tank. That was one way to use less water.

My first month on the road – adapting

Adjusting to this life might be a bit uncomfortable or scary at first. It was for me. Here are ten things I had to get used to going from a house to a van – I wrote this after six months living in a van:

1. The dark. I came from the city. I forgot how dark actual dark is. Camping in the woods on my own and in complete darkness took a bit of getting used to. I enjoy it now though.

2. Driving (really slowly) on the other side of the road. Driving a big van was new to me. And driving a big van on the other side of the road, with the steering wheel on the wrong side, was new to me. I had to get used to it. Also, the van is slow and clunky – I cruise at 55Mph max. Lorries overtake me. Sometimes people get annoyed. But I'm used to it now. I take it easy and enjoy the ride.

3. People staring. I wash in rivers, I do exercises on the floor next to my van, I eat my dinner on the floor outside. Once, a guy sat and watched me whilst taking pictures. But what's interesting is that I don't feel like people stare anymore. Maybe I got used to it, or maybe it was because I was staring at them first. Anyway, who cares.

4. Waking up wondering where I am. It took a couple of months to get used to this. I now wake up and I know I'm in my home… somewhere in Europe. Put the kettle on!

5. Knowing that everything can go wrong in a matter of seconds. This is not as safe as living in a house – breakdowns, crashes, theft, fires, leaving the gas on and forgetting to put the handbrake on are all things I worry about. I know that all my time and effort can be lost in a matter of seconds. I have to remember this and be careful. But at the same time I have to try and not let it bother me too much.

6. Being prepared to wake up and move at any time in the night. The first couple of months I'd wake up at every little sound thinking someone was going to ask me to move. But after a while I realised there was nothing to worry about.

7. Hearing and feeling every bit of weather and nature. I cannot just close the door and completely isolate myself from a thunderstorm. I feel everything. The van rocks, knocks and sometimes the door leaks – I think I've fixed it now though. If it rains hard in the night, it's loud enough to keep me awake. And the animals, they make so much noise. It's all nice noise though.

8. Not having a mirror. You can't walk through a house without seeing yourself a few times in a mirror. You don't realise until they're not there. I perfected the art of shaving in the wing mirror and cutting my own hair. But then I decided to not cut my hair at all, or shave – it's easier and warmer. I could put a proper mirror in my van but I like it without.

9. Not showering every day. It felt strange at first not being able to jump into a hot shower every morning with unlimited water. And by strange I mean dirty. But a big part of this is psychological and it's fairly easy to stay clean without showering every day – I'll explain later in the chapter, 'Toilet & washing'.

10. Digging a hole in the woods. Taking a spade into the woods and digging a hole for a toilet wasn't something I was used to. It feels normal now though. When there's a proper toilet I'm like 'woah, what an invention'.

7

Freecamping & where to stay

I love the feeling of being able to pull up to a beautiful spot –
with a view that's not even possible in a hotel – and live
there, with everything I need right here in the van. For me
this is what it's all about: having complete freedom to live
where I want. In the past couple of years I've stayed in
hundreds of amazing places, and all for free. From the wild
Carpathian Mountains of Romania to the city streets of
Athens. Last winter I camped in the Sahara Desert amongst
the sand dunes and the camels.

My plan was always to use campsites as little as possible.

Apart from being expensive, I've never seen the appeal – the fence, the noise, the rules and the cost. A mountain, river or forest is so much nicer. I built my van with this in mind: to be as autonomous as possible. I wanted to roam free and be stray. But I also wanted to be able to go into the middle of nowhere and play loud music, and shout and scream and howl and run around.

The name for this in the UK is 'wildcamping' – camping in the wilderness or in nature without a campsite or any provided amenities, and for free. Although many people use this term for any kind of camping that is free, whether it's in the actual wilderness or not. So I think 'freecamping' is more fitting because it covers everything, whether in the wilderness or in the city, so that's the term I'll use in this book.

Some other names for freecamping are: 'boondocking' or 'dry camping' (meaning without a water supply or campsite facilities) and 'stealth camping' (to camp discreetly in an urban area in a generic looking van that doesn't immediately standout as a camper).

When I moved into my van I'd heard about freecamping but had no idea how to do it. The thing that worried me is if I'd get this far only to find out that I'd constantly get told to move on by police and locals. But over the past couple of years I've never had any real problems.

So how do you freecamp? And how do you find good places? That's what this chapter is about.

Where do I stay?

The places I stay range from grim to spectacularly beautiful. It depends what I'm doing, who I'm with, where I am and what mood I'm in.

If I'm travelling and driving a lot

If I'm doing a lot of travelling over the course of a few days, I'll usually do the easiest thing and stay in a truck stop (by truck stop I just mean any roadside service station or rest stop – sometimes called 'aires' or 'aire de service' in France and Europe). These places are fine for doing the job of making dinner and having a sleep before continuing in the morning. They don't have the best views but after a full day of driving I don't always feel like going on a mission down random dirt tracks looking for a place just to spend one night. Aires and truck stops are easy to find (right by the road) and are convenient.

But if I'm travelling on the smaller roads, I'll stop in or outside a village or town. It's a bit quieter. Truck stops aren't usually the most peaceful places to sleep – and some of those truck drivers like to have a bit of a drink after work.

If I'm in a city (or village or town)

If I'm staying in a city for a while I'll look for a place that's both practical and safe. In a city this could be a carpark, gravel area, the side of a busy street, industrial area, shopping centre, sports stadium, university or residential parking.

All cities differ. Some, if you're lucky, you can find a nice quiet place right in the centre. But others you'll be lucky to find even a paid parking spot. As I write this I'm on the outskirts of Barcelona and parking is nearly impossible in the centre. But last year I stayed in Berlin for much of the summer. Berlin is like the vandweller capital of Europe. In summer the streets are lined with people living in their vans. Tables, chairs and sofas out on the grass verges. It's a lovely place to be.

I've never had any real problems camping in cities

throughout Europe. Most of the time no one bothers you, and if you have a standard looking van you blend in easily with the city scenery.

But once in Switzerland (when I'd just set off) we parked in a really rich neighbourhood. The street was massive and completely empty of cars – all the cars (Ferraris, Maseratis, etc.) were on driveways of huge mansions. We got in bed and a guy started banging on the van, going crazy and shouting. I wasn't sure if he was going to burst into tears or punch me in the mouth. I said it was no problem and we'll move. He was so mad. He wouldn't stop shouting.

Lesson: it's best not to camp in residential areas where you stand out a lot – especially when there are expensive cars and big houses. They paid a lot to live there. It spoils their view.

In less well off neighbourhoods you get given food and invited into people's homes.

If I'm in the countryside

I love the city and all the craziness and inspiration that it brings, but I can't be there for too long. When I get tired I head for nature and the countryside. It could be a national park, picnic area, nature reserve, heritage site, coast, beach, forest, mountain, lake, river or desert. The countryside offers much more freedom and variation for freecamping. This is where I stay most of the time.

Requirements of a camping spot

As the sun went down on the first night of being on the road I didn't really know what to do or where to go. I pulled over and stayed in a lay-by on the side of a busy road. I'd wake up to the van rocking every time a lorry skimmed past. I found it difficult at first to find a nice place where I could camp for free and I had no idea what would be considered an acceptable camping spot. My first few days were like this.

To give me a bit of a clue I downloaded a list of freecamping spots onto my GPS – download here: vandogtraveller.com/europe-poi-gpx. It helped me get a feel for what freecamping was like and gave me an idea of what kinds of places to look for. After a few weeks I started to develop an eye for a good spot and was able to find my own places. Here are some things I might think about when looking for a spot:

- **Does it feel safe?** The feeling of safety is subjective, and all countries are different. You may have to get to know a country before you can accurately gauge if an area is safe or not – or you can just ask local people. The best spots are when I'm in the middle of nowhere and I can sleep with the door open (in the summer), and leave stuff outside and just be relaxed.
- **Not in anyone's way.** I got in everyone's way in the beginning. Once I found a great spot on a quiet lake. No one was around. But I got woken up at 6am by an angry sailing club because I was parked right where they launch the boats. Also, what might seem like unused dirt tracks in forests are needed for local workers and also emergency services, so don't block these.
- **Can I disturb anyone?** If I want to make a lot of noise with my music I'll go further out into nature so I don't annoy anyone.
- **Quiet enough to get a good sleep.** I'm a light sleeper so I try to find somewhere fairly peaceful, and away from roads or nightlife if it's a city.
- **Not on anyone's land (or with permission if it is).** Land owners usually make it clear if they don't want you staying on their land. But sometimes, if it's a rural area you can ask if you can stay a night or two. Chances are, someone has asked them before and

they're used to it.

- **Firm ground.** Getting stuck in sand and mud is annoying. Some ground is no problem to drive on when it's dry but as soon as it rains it becomes impossible. The longest I've been stuck is three days, waiting for the ground to dry.
- **Level ground.** Sleeping on a slope gives me strange dreams. I recently put a spirit level bubble on the dashboard which helps me get the van level. If the ground isn't level I usually find a couple of rocks to put under the wheels – you can get special levelling chocks to do this but I think rocks work fine and it's less stuff to carry.
- **Will the solar panels get enough light?** If you're only staying one night this might not be a problem and there will probably be enough power in the batteries to last a day or two. I can't stay in a shaded forest for more than a few days because of this.
- **Where will the sun rise and set?** It's nice to cook and eat dinner with a view of the sunset, and have the sunrise in the morning come though the window. Sometimes you can have both.
- **A nearby water source.** If there is a water source nearby it's a big bonus and means I can stay for weeks at a time – or until my gas supply runs out.
- **Internet signal.** Some people might prefer to be totally disconnected from everything but I want to be in the middle of nowhere and still have the internet. Luckily that's not such a big ask these days with mobile internet, but there are still 'blackspots' in some areas.
- **Toilet.** If you're in the country you need somewhere (preferably a wooded area) where you can dig a hole – I'll talk about this later.

Where to look for a good spot

Finding places to stay becomes part of the adventure. It's a nice feeling when you've been driving down a dirt track for miles wondering where it's going to lead and you discover an amazing spot. Or when you find a place and it's full of vans and trucks with people cooking on fires and dogs running around and music playing. I love these little temporary communities. It's utopia. Vantopia.

After a while you'll get a feel for finding good places to stay. Here's how, and where, I look for places, whether it's for one night or one month.

Explore the grey roads

My GPS gives me three levels of road indicated by the colour: main road, residential and track. The tracks are coloured grey and only appear when you zoom in to a scale of 0.2m. These grey roads are often narrow dirt roads and can lead to some interesting places. If there are any more smaller roads off the grey roads, I'll also go down there. The idea is to keep filtering down until you get somewhere quiet and out of the way.

I've found most of my favourite places by following these roads. Exploring the grey roads at night can be exciting, and sometimes a bit scary. They can take you right into the middle of forests, to a farmer's door step, a hidden lake or off the edge of a cliff into the sea. It's lucky-dip freecamping and if you do it at night, the best surprise is in the morning when you wake up.

But these grey roads have also got me in trouble a few times. One time I got locked in a forest for two days in Austria. Another time I nearly lost the van off the edge of a narrow mountain road in Slovakia. So use these grey roads with care. They're powerful.

Safe bets

I look on the map for rivers, lakes, reservoirs, woodland, national parks, or any area coloured green on my GPS. These places are often safe bets for finding potential camping spots. If there are any grey roads going through or around these areas (there usually is) it's highly likely there will be a place to camp.

Google Earth

This can be useful for scoping out places, both city and country. A big open area of tarmac in a city is much easier to spot with Google Earth than it is with a map. And in the country you're able to see dirt roads that might not be shown in normal map view. But you can also use it to get a better general idea of what a potential spot might be like. For example, you might find what looks like a really good place but when you look at it on Google Earth it's some military or industrial zone, and so you might choose to avoid it.

Ask locals

Locals are usually more than happy to help travellers. They will know the area well and be able to tell you if it's OK to stay the night. You never know what can come from asking locals questions. You might end up having lunch with their family.

Ask other van people

You can also ask other people in vans. Maybe they've been in the area a while and they know some good places. Or you could go and find somewhere together.

Follow someone

When I don't know where I'm going in an airport I just follow someone. Same with freecamping. You can look out for other vans and follow them. This will work best around sunset when it's more likely that a van will be looking to find a place to camp for the night. I've had vans follow me also. One time I followed a van in Spain and ended up at a two-week-long rave.

Side note: If we all carried CB radios we could talk to each other, organise meetups, travel convoys, parties and just help each other out. We just need to agree on a frequency. I propose 27.115MHz – channel 13 on the US/EU citizen band.

Use a bike

Sometimes it's useful to park the van somewhere and cycle around to look for a good place to camp. This is useful in a city because you can cover an area much quicker – down small streets and one way roads, etc. I usually find places I never would have found if I was driving in the van.

Using an app

After two years of doing all of the above, someone told me about this app, Park4night. It gives you a map of all different places you can park and camp in your van. The spots are uploaded by users with a photo and description. You can even leave comments and rate each spot. I still prefer to find my own places but it's nice to have this app to fall back on. This is mainly for Europe, although I noticed some people have started to use it in the US.

For the US, there's a good website that lists loads of freecamping spots: freecampsites.net. And for Australia there's this website (also an app): wikicamps.com.au.

Camping in different countries

Some of the signs and clues that point to a good spot may work in one country but not in another. The roads, infrastructure and terrain all differ. Some countries will have masses of open land that's easily accessible from the road. In other countries it might all be bordered off with signs saying 'private'. Sometimes it can take a few days to adjust to a new country and work out any new rules and ways for finding good spots. You just have to be observant and experiment a bit.

People's attitudes also differ. In some countries you might have to be more discreet, whilst other countries it might not matter at all. It's something you'll have to gauge for yourself as you go along. If I'm not sure about staying in a place I'll just ask someone walking past. Most of the time they'll say it's not a problem, and if they're not sure they might suggest a better place near by. And if no one is walking past, it's probably not a problem.

I find that most of the countries I've been to in Europe are similar in attitude with regards to vandwelling and freecamping – relaxed and easy going. England maybe not so much.

I've found that local people will always look after you as a traveller and are often excited that you chose to visit their country. One time in Romania, a guy knocked on the van and gave me fresh goats milk and cheese. He told me to enjoy his country.

My favourite countries in Europe for van life

Spain, Portugal and Greece are all beautiful countries with amazing landscape, nature, coastline and a lot of space. They are pretty much good all year round for living in a van because of the widely varying climate. If you want to be warmer you go to the coast. If you want to be cooler you head inland – or up a mountain. I've found these countries to be very van friendly and you'll usually be able to find other vans whatever time of the year.

But there are loads of great countries for travelling in a van, and there's no such thing as a 'best country' or 'best place'. It's up to you to decide.

13 tips for happy camping

In Austria I was exploring some dirt roads through a forest as it was getting dark. I found a perfect spot in a clearing of the woods, right by a river with a view of a snow-capped mountain range. I stayed for several days but when I decided to leave there was a gate across the road. I was locked in the forest. I asked locals in the nearby village and they told me no one has the key. The gate is meant to be permanently locked. But someone must have opened it and I must have driven right through without seeing it – it was dark. Eventually the police came with a key. No problems. They were cool.

Lesson: be careful of driving through open barriers or gates. They might be open now but tomorrow they might be locked. You can often tell if a barrier is in use or not by its general condition and wear marks on the moving parts, but sometimes, if it's dark, you might not even see it, like I didn't.

Here are some more things I've learnt from freecamping in my van:

1. **Feel comfortable.** Make sure you feel fairly comfortable in the area. If you're not sure, go for a walk around and get a feel for the place.
2. **Think about the sun.** In the winter I try to point the van to the East so the sun comes through the front windscreen in the morning to warm things up. In the summer I try and point any windows away from the sun because the whole van becomes like a greenhouse.
3. **Keep fairly hidden.** If you are in the countryside, try and stay out of view from the main road and from people driving past. It keeps you out of view of police (they usually would rather you stay out of view) and opportunist thieves.

4. **Check for exits.** If it makes you feel better you can position the van in the direction of the exit incase you need to quickly get away from any danger. I've only ever had to drive away once during the night, and that was from the police in Morocco.

5. **It can get windy.** If it's seriously windy, park the van with the nose pointing into the wind – the most aerodynamic part. One time I was on a very exposed spot on a mountain side. The wind was so strong I thought the van was going to tip over the edge. I got up in the night and positioned the front of the van into the wind. It's unlikely you'll get tipped over, but it can definitely feel possible when you're inside.

6. **Careful where you park.** Be careful of parking near guard dogs, they can bark all night and keep everyone awake.

7. **Look around.** This helps to get an idea of people's attitudes. In Greece, people park in the middle of roundabouts, diagonally in the road or just wherever they feel like it. They're pretty laid back. So you can make a good guess that no one will be too bothered about a neatly parked camper van on the side of the road.

8. **City safety.** In the city it's safer to park in view of the public and in a well lit area – under a street lamp or shop lighting is good.

9. **Leave a note.** If you're leaving your van unattended in a questionable parking spot, leave a note with your name and number in the windscreen so you can be contacted in case of a problem.

10. **Don't get blocked in.** Camping in an empty parking area may fill up in the morning. Park sensibly so you don't get trapped.

11. **Be wary when you open the door.** Don't open the door to anyone without first seeing who it is.

12. **Don't throw food out near your van.** This depends where you are staying but it can attract anything

from harmless cats to wild bears.

13. **Be aware of thieves.** Thieves hang around tourist areas and camper vans can be an easy target. I usually stay away from tourist places all together. I'll talk more about securing your van in the 'Van safety' chapter.

Rules of freecamping

Basically, leave no trace. This is what I mean:

- **Take all your rubbish with you.** And anybody else's if you can.
- **Be careful of disturbing wildlife, plant life, local residents or other campers.**
- **Bury and cover any 'deposits' you make.** Always dig holes for the toilet and use 100% biodegradable tissue. I'll talk more about toilet activity later.
- **Be careful of what you dump on the ground.** No dumping detergent or any other harmful chemicals near running streams or water.
- **If you're having a fire, do it properly and safely.** Many places have a high risk of forest fires – in this case fires are usually banned all together.
- **Leave a good impression.** On people, locals, authorities or whoever. Be good and helpful and friendly to local people. I think it's important we, as a travelling community, don't get a bad reputation, otherwise laws start to happen.

About stealth camping

When I was building my van I wasn't sure how discreet I'd need to be when camping in cities – and how discreet the van would need to look. I played it safe and tried to keep the outside of it looking like a regular white van, so if I ever needed to 'stealth camp' I could. My van is moderately 'stealthy'. Most people will walk past it without thinking it's anything other than a normal van. But to another vandweller (and also police) it's probably quite obvious there's someone living in it.

It's always a good idea to be relatively discreet when camping in a city, but in Europe I've never felt the need to take it as far as full-on stealth camping. If I had to do that all the time I'd quickly get tired of it. It's a lot of effort. I've never had problems freecamping in cities all over Europe, but this will be different wherever you are in the world. Many states in the US are not tolerant of people living in their vans at all, to the point where they impose fines and legal proceedings.

So I'll share a few things you can do to be a bit more discreet. I'm not saying you should, or need to do these things. It depends where you are and the local law and attitudes.

- **Have the right van to start with.** A coach-built motorhome is clearly a motorhome, but a normal white van will easily blend into a city. This is something you have to take into account when buying or building your van. Many people build their van with the sole purpose of stealth camping.
- **Use black-out fabric.** In all windows and use dim lights inside at night.
- **Arrive at your camp spot late at night.**
- **Use a disguise.** Some city vandwellers might put signage on their van and fluorescent vests on the front seats – or anything else that will make it look like something other than a camper.
- **Park near other vehicles or vans.** Normal commercial vans with no people living inside would be best. The idea is to blend in and hide in plain sight.
- **No fires if you have a log burner.** The smoke from the chimney is a bit of a give away.
- **Stay for the minimum amount of time.** And rotate

between different spots if necessary.

- **Enter through the driver's door.** Sit there for a few minutes before climbing into the back.
- **Don't let any drain water come out onto the floor.** Even though it might be harmless water it can attract attention and kind of looks bad. This is where a grey tank can come in useful.

Like I said, I don't do any of this serious stealth camping stuff. I walk in and out of my van's side door all day long. If people look at me I just smile or say hello. So I'm not really a stealth camping expert. For more information on vandwelling and stealth camping in cities (especially in the US), there's a good community on Reddit with many long-term stealth campers who have good advice: reddit.com/r/vandwellers.

The law on freecamping

In England you're not allowed to live in your vehicle unless it's on private land with the owner's permission. And if you refuse to move on you can be detained. Section 77 of the Criminal Justice and Public Order Act 1994 (link: legislation.gov.uk/ukpga/1994/33/contents), gives a local authority the right to move you on if you are residing in a vehicle that is:

a) on any land forming part of a highway;
b) on any other unoccupied land; or
c) on any occupied land without the consent of the occupier.

In Scotland freecamping is legal and you're allowed to camp pretty much anywhere. But it's cold up there. Better in the summer.

Europe

Freecamping is technically prohibited in many European

countries but it's generally tolerated and accepted by authorities and local people. This goes for both the countryside and the city. As long as you're being respectful and not causing any harm to others or to the environment, there are no problems.

The USA

The legality and tolerance of vandwelling varies from state to state. And even if the state or locality doesn't have any explicit laws against living in a vehicle, there are several other laws (trespassing, vagrancy and loitering laws) that police commonly use against vandwellers. But most of these challenges are in urban areas and cities. The good thing is you have loads of amazing public land and national forests where you can stay, usually without problems – although I can't speak from experience here.

Dealing with police

And what do you do if police knock on the van in the night?

Most of the time, and in my experience, police are just looking out for either your safety or the safety of others. If they see a van parked in the woods they may want to check it out, just because it might look odd. Or it could be that a local resident has called the police because they are concerned or scared – let's face it, most dodgy dealings involve a white van at some point. In most of Europe, you won't have a problem opening the door to police. Once they realise you're just a harmless person living in a van they'll probably leave you to it. Driving away, just because you see police, is not a good thing to do.

But police differ in every country. In Morocco, on my first night, I got woken up by police knocking on the van. They wanted me to give them €35. I had no idea what Moroccan police were like but to me they looked shifty, leaning on the van, smoking and bickering with each other. It took me ten minutes to realise the best thing to do was to drive away. I got in the drivers seat and went. They overtook me with their blue lights on. They drove in front of me for a few miles then waved me on. I found it difficult to understand what their intention was. Were they genuinely looking out for my safety or were they trying to make a bit of money? After spending three months in Morocco I think the answer is a bit of both.

If I drove away from police in the UK, they'd chase me until I ran out of diesel and I'd get into a lot of trouble. If I did it in America they'd blow my tyres off with guns. But I drove away from police in Morocco because it didn't feel right and I felt like I should. Making these decisions isn't always easy, but most of the time, your gut will tell you what to do.

For many city vandwellers in the US it seems to be standard practice not to open the door to police. Once police can confirm there is someone in the van they'll move you on or give you a ticket. But if you don't answer the door there's nothing they can do and they usually, hopefully, have better things to do than hang around waiting for a peaceful vandweller to open the door.

But again, I don't know much about the US. I just know that in Europe it's best to answer the door to police because there is usually no problem in the first place.

Lessons from a guy who explores storm drains

There is a book I have in the van, *Access All Areas*. It has some useful tips for urban exploring – a hobby that is mostly concerned with being in places you're not meant to be. The chapter about dealing with security and authorities is potentially helpful for people living in vans – people who might have to deal with security and police more than the average person. Here's my interpretation of some of the main points:

- Authorities will be much softer on a stupid person rather than someone who is knowingly going against them and breaking the rules. Sometimes it's better to act dumb.
- See it from their point of view and show them that you do. Listen to what they say and don't interrupt.
- Make friends or make them laugh or smile or establish some common ground – without sucking up.
- Don't be in the 'me against them mindset'. We're on the same side. We need the police for our safety and protection.
- Don't be confrontational and don't contradict or argue.
- Apologise if necessary.
- Don't be a know it all. You're rarely going to win over a police officer by listing a load of legislation and law you memorised from the internet – although that doesn't mean you shouldn't know your rights.

Here's a quote I like from that book: 'People have rules against everything, unless they like you and breaking the rules would make their lives easier.'.

I'm not saying I'm good at any of this. I'm useless at 'chat'. But sometimes just listening and saying as little as possible can also go a long way. Also, the points from that book (above) are useful for dealing with anyone, not just police.

Campsites

If you ever get really stuck to find somewhere to stay you can always go to a campsite. It could be useful to have a list of campsites for the country you're going to. Or if you have the internet you can just do a search for 'camping'. Wherever you are, there's usually a campsite not far away.

The only time I've had to find a campsite was in Morocco. I was quite far south, alone near the Western Sahara border. I kept getting told by police and locals to move on. It was late and dark so I just moved a few miles each time. After the third time, I asked why I kept being asked to move. His reply, 'didn't you hear what happened in Paris?'. His friend looked at me and made the action of cutting his throat with his finger. Fair enough. I'll go to a campsite. I wasn't in a safe area. It's times like this I don't mind paying a few quid to stay in a safe campsite. I found out afterwards the area is known as 'bandit territory'. It's nice to know locals will look after you. I'm glad they told me.

Where to put your rubbish (or trash)

First of all it's best to minimise waste as much as possible in the first place. Be aware of packaging when you go shopping. Buying things in bulk (for example, dry things like rice, lentils and oats that can be stored in your own plastic containers) helps, and also buying things from local markets – way less packaging. And after that, this is what I do:

- **Use food scraps/peeling/waste to make friends with stray dogs...** or make it into a pie for tomorrow's dinner.
- **Have a separate bin (or place) in the van for plastic waste.** This is the most important thing to recycle and most countries in Europe have separate bins for plastic – they will be marked with a label or different colour.
- **Recycle cardboard and paper if possible for the country you're in.** You can also save it to use for fires.
- **For all the remaining rubbish, put it in a bin.** But

don't use bins outside people's homes. Use the large communal dumpster-type bins found pretty much everywhere in Europe – usually by the roadside or in parking areas.

- **Distribute your rubbish over a few bins.** If you're using small public bins (if you can't find the large ones), distribute the rubbish over several bins, rather than filling one bin with a whole bag of rubbish. I usually throw out rubbish as it's created rather than wait until I have a massive bag of it.

8

Toilet & washing

In this chapter I'll go over all the stuff my mum asks about: how I go to the toilet, wash and clean my clothes.

Washing and keeping clean

I used to shower every day and wash my hair every other day. If I started the day without showering I'd feel dirty, and I'd worry that I'd smell and no one would be my friend. That's the power of advertising.

But we don't need to shower every day. It's not normal or healthy. We're too clean. Frequent showering washes away the good bacteria that exists on our skin, leaving it dehydrated, irritated and more susceptible to infections. It also uses up too much of the van's water supply.

Having a proper shower might be difficult when living in a van but it's easy to stay clean, and there are plenty of ways you can get a wash. It will depend on your situation and setup, so here are a few options:

- **A gym.** All gyms provide shower facilities for their members and there are many gyms that give you access to all of their facilities nationwide. If you combine your wash with a workout you'll easily get your money's worth. In the US you have several nationwide gyms to choose from. But I've not yet found a European-wide gym.
- **Workplace.** Many workplaces have the facilities to take a shower. You may get a job whilst travelling, or maybe you plan to continue your current job whilst you're living in your van to save money for travelling. If you don't want to tell anyone at work you're living in your van, start cycling into work and say you need somewhere to shower. Or just tell them you live in a van.
- **Friend's houses.** My friend lives in her VW camper in the middle of Berlin. She goes round to different friends' houses and uses their showers in exchange for being a good friend and cooking the odd meal.
- **Truck stops.** These can be useful whilst doing a lot of travelling. Aires and motorway rest stops often have showers for travellers and truck drivers.
- **Campsites.** Some campsites may let you use the shower for free or for a small cost, but most of them you'll have to pay to stay a full night. That could soon get expensive but if you combine your stay with other things (like washing clothes, filling up with water, etc.) it could be more of a viable option

(maybe once or twice a week), depending on your money situation.

- **Communal showers in hotels.** Some of these large holiday resorts have shared showers by the pool and it's quite easy to just sling a towel over your shoulder and walk in. No one knows who is staying there and who isn't. But this is kind of stealing, so it isn't something I'm recommending.
- **The beach.** Outdoor showers are usually provided along beaches. It's cold water but a good option in the summer.
- **In nature.** The sea, river, streams and hot springs. But only use environmentally safe soap, or none at all.
- **Solar shower.** This is basically just a black vinyl bag with a tap and small flexible shower head at the bottom. They cost about £15. You fill it with water and leave it out in the sun to warm up. Hang it on a tree or on the back door of the van and have a shower. You can have a surprisingly decent shower with one of these.
- **Bottle shower.** If you don't have a camping shower you can make your own. Fill a two litre bottle with water and put some holes in the lid. Hold it above your head and shower – use the other hand for washing and then swap hands. Dark coloured bottles work better to absorb the heat for warming the water up, or you can cover it in black tape. Keep the bottle cap in your van and you can screw it onto any bottle – it's a shower you can fit in the palm of your hand. Credit to my friend Matt for this idea.
- **Shower in your van.** I have a shower in my van that's heated with an instant gas boiler. It works well but water is limited and it doesn't last long, so to conserve water I have a 'navy shower' – I'll explain that in a second.
- **Bucket wash.** Stand in a bucket and wash down with

a cloth or sponge. You can easily do this in any van and it's probably the best way to have a decent wash if you don't have a shower in your van.

- **Wet wipes.** I use wet wipes on the critical areas throughout the day. It's a waste of water to wash the bits that don't need washing. Elbows never smell.

To get a proper wash I use the shower in my van. This is a built in wet room with a toilet and shower – photos are on the blog if you haven't seen it. To save water I use the 'navy shower' technique: wet your body (about 20 seconds of water), turn the water off whilst you lather up, then rinse (maybe about 30 seconds of water). The aim is to keep water flow to the minimum, only turning the tap on when it's needed. The most useful thing for washing like this is one of those shower scrunchie things – or a 'shower pouf' – I don't know the proper name. A sponge is also good because it holds a lot of water.

Also, if you have a shower in your van you can get an 'eco' shower head that uses less water. Some of these work by pulsing the water on and off, and others work by simply restricting the flow of water. You can do a DIY version of this by fitting a jubilee clip around the pipe to restrict the water flow – assuming the pipe is the flexible type, as it is in most van conversions.

As for washing hair, I do that in the sink, and no more than once a week. By not using shampoo I'm able to wash my hair much less often, saving even more water. I'll explain.

Why I don't use shampoo

We use shampoo because we get greasy hair. But we get greasy hair because we use shampoo. If you shampoo your hair regularly it strips the scalp of its natural oils making it overreact, producing excess oils to compensate – greasy hair.

So we use shampoo again to get rid of the grease. The cycle continues. And then we have to use a conditioner to replace the natural oils, that the powerful detergents in the shampoo stripped away, with artificial ones.

On top of this, shampoo contains some of the most harmful chemicals that we use on our skin. I'd rather save the money, water, time, have healthier hair and maybe do a little bit less damage to the environment. So I don't use shampoo. I think hair is meant to look glossy and healthy on its own. Like a dog.

You can either just stop using shampoo or slowly phase it out. It takes a while for your scalp and hair to go back to it's natural state, and this is when people revert back to shampoo, but I think it's worth the wait– it took me about five months. I've not used shampoo now for nearly two years.

How do I wash my hair? I use Moroccan Rhassoul clay and rinse it with a cap full of vinegar and water. This works well for me and my hair hardly gets greasy anymore, even if I leave it two weeks or more. There are loads of alternatives you can use to wash your hair, and there's a whole Facebook group dedicated to the 'nopoo' way of life. See facebook.com/groups/nopoo.

What about the toilet?

The thought of not being without a fixed flushable toilet is a bit worrying at first. We're so used to always having a toilet, we don't even think about it, and it's not something we particularly want to think about. But now you live in a van, you have no choice. It's not much of a problem though.

Here's how I see it. If you are in or near a city, there will always be a toilet near by – in shops, cafes, public toilets, etc.

If you are in the countryside, there are toilets, but you might have to dig a hole. I think everything is a lot easier if you're staying in nature. You can pee pretty much anywhere and dig a hole for everything else. This might feel strange at first but you get used to it. You might even start preferring it to a proper toilet – the view will almost certainly be better.

So now I'll go through some of the ways to deal with the toilet situation when living in a van. This will depend on what facilities you have, and also where you're staying.

In the city

There are many places in the city where you can use a toilet. Apart from public toilets, McDonalds always has nice facilities and for some reason I don't feel so guilty about using them without buying anything. If they have staff guarding the bathroom door to check you are a customer, just take a receipt from a table and show it to them. No problem.

If you're staying in the city for a while, you could get to know some people and make some agreement to use their toilet. In Berlin I camped next to a 'Wagonplatz' for most of the summer and had use of their outdoor compost toilet.

But if you're in the city and you need the toilet in the night, you'll need a way to go in your van. So now I'll go through some of the toilet options.

A toilet in your van

My van has a built-in 'cassette toilet' (Thetford C-200CW). It has a tank in the top that you fill with water for the flush water, which is operated with a hand pump. The waste drops down, along with the rinse water, into a removable container (the cassette) that's assessed and removed from outside, at the back of my van. When it's full you remove the cassette and empty it into a toilet or at a disposal point.

This is where having a toilet in my van is really useful. I can just get up in the night and use it like I would in a house. No hassle. It's also useful for when I have friends staying over. But if your van doesn't have a built-in toilet already, the other option is a Porta Potti.

Porta Potti

This is very similar in operation to the toilet above, having a tank for flush water and a removable tank in the bottom for the waste. The only difference is that this is portable, and also much cheaper. If you don't already have a toilet in your van, this is a good solution and can fit easily into an existing van conversion.

In Europe the most well known brand for these kinds of toilets is Thetford. To see an example of one of these have a look at the product listings on my blog – the link is at the beginning of this book. Or Google 'Thetford Qube toilet'.

About toilet chemicals

The two toilets I just mentioned above are designed to be used with chemicals to help keep things clean, break down the waste and neutralise any smells. You put one kind of chemical in the flush water (usually pink in colour) and another in the waste tank (usually blue or green in colour).

But some of these chemicals are not so friendly. Not only do you have to be careful handling them but you have to be absolutely sure you can dispose of them properly. In many of these products, formaldehyde is the main active compound. Remember when Damien Hirst cut a cow into sections and put it in a glass box so everyone could see? He used formaldehyde for that. It's highly toxic and can cause all sorts of problems for humans and wildlife. If you must use chemicals, there are much safer alternatives (without formaldehyde) available and will usually say 'non-toxic' or 'eco-friendly' on the label.

Nowadays I don't bother using any chemicals at all. When I'm in the van I only use my toilet for peeing – it's less messy and smelly and easier to empty – so there's no need to use chemicals. Every now and then I'll just wash the cassette out with warm water and white vinegar.

A bucket toilet

Some van people might make a DIY toilet out of a bucket. You line it with a plastic bag, do your business, tie it up and chuck it in a bin. But it's best not to pee in here, you have to do that separate. You can put something around the rim of the bucket (like foam pipe lagging) to make it more comfortable to sit on. Or you could fit a plastic toilet seat to the bucket – you can even buy special toilet seats in camping shops that are designed to fit onto a bucket. To give you some ideas, do a Google search for 'DIY camping toilet'.

But for £60 or so, I think a Porta Potti is a much better solution – it's easier to store and more sanitary. If you prefer you can just use the Porta Potti for peeing only, and use the bag method (mentioned above) for solid waste. And as an eco-friendly alternative to plastic bags, you can get starch bags. They are made from 100% vegetable starch, making them completely biodegradable and compostable – you can throw them straight onto a compost heap. They're a bit more expensive (about £6 for 100) but the price will soon drop as they start to replace plastic bags.

Compost toilet

My friends have a compost toilet in their van. They use a bucket filled with sawdust, or any organic matter like leaves, twigs, soil, etc. When it's full they empty it into their allotment, which is just down the road. In return they get free carrots, leeks, parsnips, onions and all sorts. But this kind of arrangement is only good whilst staying in the same place, unless you have some kind of vegetable plot on the roof of the van – I've been meaning to do this. Although, I don't see a problem with going into the woods to properly bury the compost.

Going outside – when in nature

If you've ever been camping you'll know what to do here. You'll need a small shovel or trowel. Or you can get folding spades that are a bit easier to store in a van, and easier to put in your bag or jacket pocket. So here's how to shit in the woods:

1. **Find a spot.** It should be away from water, trails/paths or camping sites (at least 60m). Try to find rich organic soil like in woodland and forested areas. The aim is to find a place for maximum decomposition.
2. **Dig a hole.** With the hole at least six inches deep, squat down and do your business.
3. **Use only biodegradable toilet paper.** You can either bury it, burn it or dispose of it somewhere else. But be careful of burning it – I read about a cyclist who accidentally started a 70 acre forest fire after burning his toilet paper, but that was probably just bad luck. Also, most wet wipes are not biodegradable so don't bury those.
4. **Bury.** Use the loose soil you dug up to fill in the hole and bury it. It's important that animals don't dig it back up and spread it around, so make sure it's properly buried and flattened.

If you're camping in the same place for a while, or with other people, you can dig a latrine (aka shit pit). It's the same as the above (at least six inches deep) but extended in length, and you'd usually have it pre-dug to make it easier for everyone. You start from one end, covering over with soil until it's full.

Random fact about squatting

Everyone used the squatting position until the second half of the 19th century. There has been a lot of research into the benefits of going to the toilet in the squatting position, as opposed to the sitting position. They've linked the sitting position to many of the common health problems we see today, including colon cancer and inflammatory bowel disease. There's also more chance of having a stroke or heart attack when doing your business in the sitting position. Forget a high fibre diet, maybe squatting is the answer. How true this is I don't know. RIP, Elvis.

About peeing – when in nature

If I'm in the countryside I just pee anywhere. But it's best to do it away from water or running streams, and it's best not to pee in the same place all the time because it'll eventually start to smell. Urine is a soil enhancer and rich in nitrogen. So spread it around fairly.

If I'm camping in nature and I need a pee in the middle of the night, I'll usually still go outside, even though I have a toilet in my van. I've had some deeply insightful moments when I've woken up in the night and gone outside to pee. I'll stand barefoot in my boxer shorts, all alone, looking up at the sky, the stars, the moon. It's totally surreal. I enjoy it. I also enjoy getting back into my warm bed and falling back into the same dream.

How to wash clothes

Here are some places you can go to wash your clothes:

- **Hotels or hostels.** You don't have to be staying there. Traveller's hostels will usually be able to help you or at least point you towards the washing machines that they use.
- **Couchsurfing.** You can find someone local using the

Couchsurfing website and ask if you can use their washing machine, offering them some favour in return.

- **Self-service laundrettes.** Even though most people have a washing machine in their homes, laundrettes still exist and people still use them. I've met some cool people whilst sitting in a laundrette. I like it. It's where I'll meet my future wife.
- **In the van.** Using a bucket or the sink – I'll explain that now.

If I have a lot of things to wash, like bedding, cushion covers, curtains and clothes, I'll go to the laundrettes. But most of the time I wash my clothes in the sink or in a 20L bucket. I'll usually try to wash items as and when they need washing, rather than waiting until there's a big pile. On a nice day, and with a bit of music, sitting on the step of the van and washing clothes can be an enjoyable thing to do. To dry them I either lay them flat on the van's mesh roof-rack, or tie a washing line between the van and a tree.

There are a few devices and gadgets designed to help you wash clothes with no power and minimal water. One of them is the the Drumi foot powered washing machine. It uses a small amount of water and requires no electricity – the drum spins by compressing a foot pedal. It's a nicely designed product but, for me, it would take up too much space in my van for the minimal use it would get. I think a simple bucket wash is more effective – you can see what you're washing and scrub at any stains that need to come out. And I use the bucket to store things when I'm not using it for washing.

If you're hand washing clothes like this, you have to be careful where you're dumping the detergent water. Always make sure you are well away from any water or running streams. The best bet is to use an eco-friendly detergent – it's also better on your skin. One of these products is Ecos

Laundry Detergent, which is free from all of the harmful chemicals found in normal detergents.

Another detergent alternative, and one that is 100% natural, is Indian soapnut – also called soapberries. It's an all-natural plant-based product you can use to wash your clothes, and it's completely friendly on the environment. It's basically just a dried berry, about one inch in diameter, from a soapnut tree. They contain saponin, a natural detergent, and have been used for centuries for washing pretty much anything. To use soapnuts, put a few in a cotton draw-string bag and drop it in the bucket with your washing. You can reuse the same soapnuts a few times before they loose their soapiness.

You can buy soapnuts online (amazon) and they can even work out cheaper than detergent. You could even grow your own soapnut tree, but it'll take about nine years to fruit. And the only other downside is that you can't eat them.

9

Cooking & eating

Living in a van doesn't mean you have to eat pasta out of a pan every night. I've not done that since I lived in a house. Cooking in a kitchen on my own in the back of my house with a view of a brick wall was boring. But cooking in the outdoors with a view, and music, and people, is the best. I love it.

Since living in my van I eat a much better diet. I'm much more conscious of the food I eat and the effect it has on me. I think you're almost forced to eat better. You're away from all that fast-paced quick snack lifestyle and there's time to cook good food and properly taste what you're eating. It sounds obvious but I didn't do that before.

But a van kitchen does have its limitations. If you're used to having a full kitchen, like in a house, some adjustments have to be made, often with a bit of creative problem solving.

Limitations of a van kitchen

Here are a few of the kitchen limitations that you'll probably face when living in a van. Depending on your setup you might just have one or two of these, or all of them:

- **No microwave.** They simply take too much power for most van's electrical systems.
- **No oven.** It is possible to have a gas oven in your van, and many larger motorhomes do, but in a normal van it usually takes up too much space.
- **Limited electrical appliances.** Toaster, kettle, blenders and mixers, coffee makers, etc. They take up too much power for most van electrical systems.
- **Limited fridge and storage space.** It might mean you have to change your shopping habits slightly – for example, you might have to buy food more often, especially fresh things.

Generally speaking, anything that uses electricity to make something spin at high speed, or to heat something up, will use too much power in a van. There are ways round this but it just depends how much you feel you need that gadget or device. My friends have a blender in their van so they can make their own houmous. But the van's engine has to be running to get enough power to blend the chickpeas – they use a volt sensing relay to get power from the alternator. It's not the most economical way to run a blender but it is good houmous.

For cooking in my van, I have two gas hobs. But you can do a lot with just two hobs and I've never missed having an oven. I think the combination of limited facilities (and limited money) forces you to be more creative. I've become a much better cook since living in a van. I think. Although I do miss cheese on toast a little bit. A grill would be useful – possible future upgrade.

Kitchen equipment

Like with everything else, the key is to have only what you need and use. And if something can perform two functions then it's a bonus. This is what I have in my kitchen:

- **Pans:** frying pan, saucepan and a big stew pot. Lids are useful to reduce steam and save energy.
- **Clay tagine pot:** for cooking in a fire.
- **A simple flat grater.** Those big four sided ones take up too much space.
- **Foldable steamer.** I mainly use this as a colander to drain rice and pasta.
- **Whistling kettle.** The cheap aluminium camping kettles are not worth bothering with and they break quickly. A good quality stainless steel or copper one is much better.
- **Cutlery.** Just enough, not a draw full. I use a large knife magnet that's fixed inside the draw so things don't rattle around when driving.
- **Chopping board.** Mine's large enough to fit over the kitchen sink which gives me a bit of extra surface space whilst cooking.
- **Utensils:** wooden spoon, spatula and big serving spoon.
- **Plastic measuring jug:** for mixing ingredients.
- **Large plastic bowl:** for making salads and mixing.
- **Selection of Tupperware:** for storing left over food and ingredients.

- **Corkscrew/bottle opener.**
- **Tin opener.**
- **A supply of matches and lighters** – they always get lost.
- **Miscellaneous kitchen items:** tin foil, cling film, kitchen towels and squirt bottle for cleaning – I fill this with white vinegar and water.

Food for van living

I'll go over the essentials food items I keep in my van, and where I store it all.

Dry things

Dry things can be easily stored and last a long time. I probably stock up on these things no more than once a month: lentils, beans, brown rice, brown pasta, couscous, wheat, barley, quinoa, seeds and nuts. I use at least one of these items as a staple in my meals and it's all kept in a plastic container that slides out from under the sofa bed.

Tinned things

I also like to keep a good stock of tinned food. It takes years before it goes out of date and even after that it's still good. My tinned essentials are: fish (sardines, herring or tuna), beans and pulses, chick peas, chopped tomatoes and coconut milk. I keep tins on the bottom shelf of my kitchen unit and in any other spare bit of space they can fit.

Fresh things

I usually buy fresh things once or twice a week, depending on where I am. Buying in-season local produce, and away from tourist areas saves money. Fresh essentials include: onions, garlic, ginger, pepper, eggs, cheese, spinach, tomatoes and a selection of fruit.

I keep vegetables in two plastic baskets on a shelf in the

kitchen cupboard. I put an anti-slip mat on the shelves so nothing falls off when I'm driving – it works really well. Fruit is kept in a metal basket that's hung under the kitchen shelf. All the other fresh stuff is in my fridge. It's a Waceo CDF-18 compressor fridge that runs on 12V. They are great fridges and consume very little power. The temperature can be set manually and you select either freezer or fridge mode, but not both.

Spices and herbs

I keep a store of spices and herbs in the dry food box under the sofa bed. I use this to top up the small jars in the spice rack (above the kitchen sink) when needed. My spice rack is always changing, but the essentials include: turmeric, cumin, paprika, oregano and basil.

Condiments and everything else

This is all the random (but essential) things like: pesto, soy sauce, stock cubes, mayonnaise, salt, pepper, honey, curry paste, oil, apple cider vinegar or balsamic, and Marmite. I keep all this stuff on the main kitchen shelf that's easily accessible whilst cooking.

What do I eat in my van?

I don't have names for any of the meals I cook. I just make it up as I go along. It also depends what country I'm in, what food I have in the van and what music I'm listening to. The contents of the pan usually resembles risotto, vegetable thingy or some kind of curry. It's all very simple cooking. Here's what I'll typically eat in my van.

Breakfast: Muesli with yoghurt or a handful of nuts and some fruit. Or my favourite breakfast: eggs, whole grain bread, Marmite, avocado, tomatoes and spinach.

Lunch: Greek salad, Spanish omelette, tinned fish or just leftover food that needs eating.

Dinner: It usually goes something like this. In the large frying pan I put in some fresh vegetables with some spices. I like to eat a variety of colours, so I choose what food to put in the pan by its colour. If there's no red in there, I'll put in a red pepper. In the saucepan I put some kind of grain, pulse or legume, or combination of. As a side dish I'll have some leaves (usually rocket or spinach) with tomato, feta and oil. That's it. It's all pretty basic, but good basic.

Dessert (I call it pudding): Sometimes I'll make pancakes. It's an easy and cheap sweet snack to cook in a van. Other cheap puddings include homemade rice pudding (rice and milk), banana and custard, sugar on pan-bread and yoghurt with honey.

Snacks: I like to keep a good stock of snacks in the van to eat throughout the day. Things like: mixed nuts, dark chocolate, crackers, fruit, seeds, bread and cheese.

About pan-bread

It's possible to cook flat bread – and even pizza – in a pan on the hob. The trick is to get a frying pan (or wok) with a lid. Use flour instead of oil and get the pan hot before you put the dough in. You can make all sorts of bread – with herbs, cheese, garlic or spices, nuts, vegetables or whatever. You can even make cookies like this, and other weird creations.

My favourite recipes from The Camper Van Cookbook

Before moving into my van, I picked up a copy of *The Camper Van Cookbook* by Martin Dorey. It has over 80 van-friendly recipes that you can cook on two rings, along with loads of other practical tips and photos.

I sent Martin an email the other day asking if I could share a few of my favourite recipes from his book. He said go for it. Thank you, Martin. So here are three of my favourites:

Thai Lentil and coconut soup (page 118)

For 4-6:

- 1 tbsp oil
- 2 tbsp of Thai green curry paste
- 2 large Carrots (about 300g), peeled and chopped small
- 2 medium Parsnips (about 250g), peeled and chopped small
- 1 x 400ml tin coconut milk
- 400ml chicken or vegetable stock
- 1 x 400g tin of green lentils, drained
- 4 generous handfuls young leaf spinach

Heat the oil in a medium to large saucepan and stir in the curry paste, carrots and parsnips. Cook over the heat for about 10 minutes, stirring now and then. Pour in the coconut milk and stock and bring to boil. Reduce the heat and simmer the soup, partially covered, for 15 minute or until the chopped vegetables are just tender.

Stir in the lentils and bring back to the boil. Add salt to taste. Add half the spinach, stir until wilted, then add the other half and as soon as that has wilted, ladle into mugs or bowls.

Greek salad (page 107)

For 6:

- 200g (about 275ml) couscous
- 1 tbsp olive oil
- Quarter of a cucumber
- 2 tomatoes
- 200g feta
- Half a red onion
- Zest and juice of 1 lemon
- 2-3 tbsp of chopped parsley
- 1-2 tbsp of chopped mint
- Sprinkle of dried or fresh oregano (or thyme)
- Handful of olives (optional)

Tip the couscous into a bowl, drizzle with the olive oil and pour over 350ml boiling water. Leave to soak for 5 minutes or so, Chop the cucumber, tomatoes and feta. Peel and thinly slice the onion. Toss the couscous with these and all the other ingredients.

Rocky Road (page 69)

Makes 16 squares:

- 150g of butter
- 4 tbsp of golden syrup or runny honey
- 400g of milk chocolate, broken up into squares
- 10 pink and white marshmallows (about 100g)
- 12 digestives or other oatmeal biscuits (about 150g)
- 20 glace cherries (about 100g)
- 4 tbsp sultanas

In a pan over a low heat, gently melt the butter with the golden syrup or honey and the chocolate. Cool the mixture while you chop the rest of the ingredients.

Chop the marshmallows and biscuits and quarter the cherries. Stir these and the sultanas into the chocolate mixture and mix together. Tip the mixture into a lightly buttered 20cm, shallow-sided square cake tin (or similar-sized dish –we used a handy Tupperware box). Cool and chill to set, 2-3 hours should do it. Cut into chunky squares – or bars if you prefer.

All the above recipes are taken from *The Camper Van Cookbook* by Martin Dorey and Sarah Randell published by Saltyard Books in 2011.

Outside cooking

The first Christmas I had on the road, when I was in Athens, my family came to see me. We had a fire on the beach with music, wine and food that we just bought from the local market. It was so simple and it cost just €10 per person. The best Christmas yet – that's the photo at the beginning of this chapter.

It's also nice when there's a communal fire going and everyone cooks something different, adding to the feast. I love the summer. There are several ways to cook in the fire:

- **Clay tagine.** You put all the ingredients in at once with some simple spices and stick it in the fire – Moroccan style.
- **Metal griddle.** Good for cooking fish and grilling vegetables. It's useful to keep one of these in the van, preferably one with handles.
- **Pans and pots.** You can use your normal kitchen pots on the fire if you want, but be careful of burning any plastic handles.
- **Foil.** You can wrap anything (vegetables are usually good) in foil with some herbs, spices, garlic and put it in the hot embers. But this is a bit of a last resort. Note: aluminium might not be so good to cook food in on a regular basis – Google will tell you some of the (debatable) health risks.

In Morocco, I was completely alone in the wilderness under the pitch-black night sky. I made a fire. It was so silent and the stars were amazing, like a display that was just for me. I'd bought a fish earlier in the day from a guy on a donkey. I gutted it by the fire light and cooked it on the glowing embers with some vegetables. Simple and primitive. It's times like this when I think THIS is living. Why does everything have to be so complicated? Happiness is simple and easy. Perspective gets adjusted in these moments. But yeah, I did feel a bit guilty gutting that fish.

Wild food

In Hungary me and my friend were camped next to a plum tree. We filled bags full of plums. Then we found a box full of glass jars, and a sachet of unopened cinnamon in a nearby bin. We made enough plum jam to last for months. Great on porridge. And yeah, we did wash the jars out before we used them.

There's loads of edible food that grows in abundance all around us and it's easy to forget about:

- **Mushrooms.** There are thousands of mushrooms that grow at all different times of the year. Most mushrooms are edible, but some might give you a bad stomach and others will kill you. With mushrooms, it's best to know what you're doing.
- **Leaves and herbs.** Wild mint, thyme, fennel and nettle.
- **Fruit and berries.** Rosehip, blackberries, brambles, apples, oranges, lemons and plums pretty much grow everywhere. I'll often stop the van to collect a few lemons or oranges off the floor.

There are plenty of foraging books that will show you what food grows in your region. There's a good one in the UK called *Wild Food* by Roger Phillips, which also includes recipes.

How to get free food

About one third of all food produced in the world (about 1.3 billion tonnes) is wasted every year. Supermarkets make up a large part of this. If any food is a bit damaged or 'abnormal' looking, or just approaching its sell by date, it's thrown away even though it's perfectly fine to eat.

One time (before living in a van) I gave a homeless guy a cheese and pickle sandwich. He looked at the packet and told me he didn't like pickle. I wondered how he could be so fussy. But now I know. It's because he has the choice of whatever sandwich he wants round the back of Tesco.

Here are some ways you can get free food:

- **Bins.** Supermarkets throw away some amazing food and a lot of it is in its unopened packaging just a day or two out of date. Once you work out the best times when they throw out the food, you're laughing. For more information on 'dumpster diving' check out http://trashwiki.org. It might be illegal but it's definitely not wrong (what is wrong is to waste the food) and you're not going to get into much trouble if you get caught.
- **Ask in shops.** Fresh bakery goods cannot be kept for long. Many places will throw out or give away a lot of these things at the end of the day.
- **Markets.** It's best to come just before the stalls are packing up. You can either collect food off the floor or ask if there's any food that's going to be thrown away. If they say no, offer to help them pack away in exchange for a few vegetables.
- **The end of festivals.** You can get weeks' worth of shopping at the end of festivals. You can have a huge feast – and a whole party – from all the stuff left behind.

In Greece, whilst staying at the 'Jedi Academy' (a crazy place where people from all over the world come and go, living together communally in an old cafe on top of a hill) we'd team up twice a week to do food missions into the nearby town (using the first three methods above). We'd always come back with loads of food – bags of beautifully made bread, expensive homemade Greek sweets and boxes full of fruit and vegetables. We were feeding up to 20 people every night, all for free. To see my post on getting free food, search the blog for 'free food'.

I spent a good part of my first year living like this, eating food that was going to waste. If you don't have much money, it's good to know there's always a way to get food. I don't do this any more, because I don't need to, and some people rely on this as their only supply of food.

A happy van kitchen

Here are some things I do to have a happy van kitchen:

- **Wash up straight away.** As soon as I'm finished with my plate I wash it without even realising. It's a good habit to make and it saves water – washing dried food off plates takes a lot more washing.
- **Tidy as you cook.** As soon as I'm finished with something it goes back in its place. There's no room to have everything out. By the time I'm finished cooking, most things are already cleaned and put away. I never used to be this tidy, but living in a van has forced me to be.
- **No food down the sink.** The drain can quickly get smelly and food gets trapped in the corrugated waste pipe.
- **Careful of condensation build up.** Use the extractor fan and open vents or windows to let the steam out. I usually cook with the side door of my van open as it's right next to the kitchen.
- **Watch CO (carbon monoxide) levels.** Especially if you have a gas oven that's being left on to slow cook something for some time.
- **Cook really smelly stuff outside (like fish or curry).** Or at least with doors and windows open.
- **Have a fire blanket at the ready.** Hot oil can burst into flames, and in an enclosed space like a van, flames catch easily. I'll talk a bit more about van safety in the next chapter.

10

Van safety

If you're living in a van and travelling, you're opening
yourself up to new risks that were not there before in
'normal' life. It's a bit of a trade we have to make. But from
my experience it's not such a bad deal and I've not had much
trouble so far. Most of the time I feel very safe. But these new
risks are still there and we have to be aware of them so we
can minimise them where possible. That's what I'll talk
about in this chapter.

Who's at the door?

I mentioned in the 'Freecamping & where to stay' chapter

that you should always have a look to see who is at the door before opening it. In my van I have a window in the side door which is really useful for this – and that's the door most people knock on. But it can be a tense moment when a stranger knocks on the door. You have to make a decision whether or not to open it, and all you have to base your decision on is what that person looks like. I can't really tell you how to do that but, as humans, I think we're generally very good at making these split-second visual judgments. So listen to your gut.

One time I'd just got into bed and there was someone banging on the van. There was an odd-looking guy outside. I didn't open it at first. But then I did. He just wanted some food. So I made him a sandwich and a drink. Then I went back to bed.

Another time, I was camping alone on a deserted part of the Moroccan coast. Some guy appeared out of nowhere asking for a knife. He seemed alright – he was old and only one of his eyes seemed to work – so I gave him the big knife. He came in, sat down, cut up a large block of opium, thanked me and was on his way.

Some of these people might seem scary at first. But they're just humans trying to live and make a living. The world isn't full of psychopaths and murderers. The news is mostly made up. The vast majority of people are cool.

Animals

You're probably more likely to get beaten up by an animal than a human. In Bulgaria I got chased by wild dogs. They weren't like the dogs that I was used to. They were monsters. I made the mistake of running away. They chased me. I looked back and they were ready to kill. I thought I was dead. One of them caught me by the jeans and his tooth ripped them like a razor, right up to my hip. I got away with just a graze, but the image of those monster dogs played over in my mind for weeks after. I can still see all those teeth and spit.

The lesson: don't run from wild dogs, or guard dogs, because they will chase you. Instead, bend down as if to pick up a rock and don't turn your back on them. They will back off.

Since then, I've made friends with wild dogs. If you get on their good side they can protect you. I recently had two dogs that slept next to the van every night for three weeks. They would bark when people went past.

Another thing to watch out for is wild boar. Especially if you go outside of the van at night to pee. They can charge at you and they're quite vicious.

Bears also. In many parts of the world (including Europe), bears are a danger, especially to people camping or hiking. When I was in Romania I went looking for bears in the Carpathian Mountains. I found one of their hideouts. I was close. But I was alone and I hadn't told anyone where I was going. I remembered a story of a guy's wife getting eaten right in front of him on this same mountain range, so I ran back to the van. Two hours later I came face to face with a big brown bear, just a few metres away. We looked at each other for about 20 seconds. I was lucky I was sat in my van this time.

If you're going anywhere where there are bears, know what you're doing and know what to do if you come face to face with one. But most of the time the bear will be long gone after hearing your footsteps. So if you're walking into bear territory make lots of noise to warn them. Clap your hands and sing as you walk.

The thief

Your van is your home with all your stuff inside and it can be broken into and driven away. It's a scary thought and it's one of the main things that worries me. Most of the time though, a thief will break in to take a single item of value, rather than the whole van. That's not to say it doesn't happen, but it's much easier, and more profitable, to just take a MacBook or camera to make a quick few quid.

A thief will always target the easiest option. If you leave something of value on show in your van, a thief knows for definite that if they break the glass they will get it, so it's fairly low risk for them. All we can do is make things a bit more difficult so we are not the easiest target.

Secure your van and deter thieves

Here are a few things you can do to make your van safer and a bit more secure. You may choose to do a couple of these things or all of them.

Install a tracker

There are several different vehicle tracker products you can get. The idea is that if the car gets stolen you'll be able to track its location remotely through your computer or phone. Trackers are small devices that have a built in GPS satellite receiver and communicate to you via the mobile cellular network, so they'll need a registered sim card to work.

I installed a GPS tracker when I first converted my van. I made a review of it and documented the installation on one of my early blog posts – search the blog for 'GPS tracker'. The great thing about this tracker is that it can alert you (via a text message) when any doors have been opened on the van, or if the engine has been started. It has many different features and can even trigger an audible siren – more than just a tracker. It's one of these no-brand products but the model (as sold on Amazon) is 'TK103A'.

Alarm system

Sometimes a loud siren sound might be enough to deter a casual thief – especially in a busy area. You can get these quite cheap. My friends have a proper house alarm system in their bus with infrared sensors covering every area. It's always going off.

Improve existing locks

The weak point on a vehicle, apart from a window, is the locks. Standard locks, especially on older vans, are not so good. With a flat screwdriver you can push it behind the lock face plate to manipulate the linkage rod and open the door. But there are after-market products you can fit to protect against this. It's usually some kind of steel plate that fits around the existing lock, preventing a screwdriver getting underneath it. You can buy a set of these to fit your specific model of van. Do a Google search for 'van lock plates'.

Install deadlocks

I installed deadlocks to all the doors of my van (the front cab doors, side door and rear doors) to make it more secure. These are the kind of locks you find in modern houses and are very difficult to break. Now, the only way to get into my van would be to smash one of the windows. But with the window broken, the thief would not be able to reach inside the door and unlock it (like they normally would) because the deadlock can only be locked and unlocked with the key. He'd have to climb through the broken window and he'd get all cut – hopefully making it too difficult to bother.

I got my deadlocks from a company in the UK, Locks4Vans, who sell lock kits to fit pretty much every type of van. They are high quality locks and come with detailed fitting instructions. To see a photo of these locks, and details of how I fitted them, search the blog for 'deadlocks'.

Fit a disarm switch

Some people fit an ignition inhibit switch, mounted in some hidden place around the driver's seat or under the dashboard. This switch would be wired in series with one of the ignition wires or a control voltage wire to the starter motor relay or fuel pump. So if someone was able to get in the van and hot-wire it, they'd still have to find the hidden switch to get the engine to start.

Install a safe

You might want to install a safe in your van to keep valuable possessions. You can have it fixed to the solid structure of the van's floor so it cannot be removed. The only problem is that it tells the thief exactly where your valuables are. And also, safes are not so big – I couldn't fit my computer in there and that's my most valuable thing. I'd rather have several secret hiding spots instead.

Secret hiding spots

Most thieves breaking into a van will look in the obvious places and then make a run with what they can. So it's a good idea to have random hiding spots for valuables. The more obscure, the better. You could even combine hiding spots with a safe. But have the safe empty (and locked), so it's just a distraction – a thief will spend most of their time trying to open it. Anything to trick or deceive a thief will slow them down a lot.

Decoy items

You could keep one of your old smartphones, or other semi-valuable bits of technology that you no longer use, in an obvious place (but not visible from outside the van) like a drawer or cupboard. If the thief finds a smartphone in the draw they'll just swipe it and run, whilst your diamond encrusted iPhone 11 is hidden in a box of muesli. Or whatever.

Never leave your van unlocked

Thieves target places where people might leave their vehicles unlocked – like service stations, lay-bys and pay and display car parks. In the city, no matter how little time you'll be away from your van, even if it's 20 seconds, always lock it.

Never leave anything on show

When people have their vans broken into it's nearly always because they have left something valuable in sight – a phone on the seat, a laptop in the side of the door or just a bit of a camera strap showing from under the seat. Even when you are in your van, try to minimise what people can see from outside. As soon as you stop the van to park up, move everything out of sight immediately – the GPS and iPod, etc. Even signs of things like phone chargers, iPod cables or a GPS holder on the windscreen will help a thief choose what van or car to break in to.

Don't underestimate the chances a thief will make

Even if you are in a proper carpark or somewhere in clear view of the public it doesn't mean a thief will not take the chance of breaking into your van to take something valuable. City thieves work quickly and are highly skilled. And many people in big cities will not intervene, or even bat an eyelid, when they walk past a thief breaking into a van. Thieves know this.

Always be cautious

If I'm in a city and I'm walking back to my van, I will never hold anything of value (like my camera or computer) in my hands. I'll put any valuable stuff in my bag way before I approach my van. In cities, thieves are always around, watching. Building in little habits like this should greatly reduce the chances of you being a target.

Locking yourself out of the van

Your van is your home and your transport, so locking yourself out would not be cool. But if this ever happens to you, you'll want to be able to get back in, preferably without breaking anything. I mentioned earlier about the time I locked myself out of my van. First, I'll explain how I got back in.

I got a wooden triangle block (shaped like a door wedge) and a bit of flexible PVC conduit I found in a nearby skip. I wedged the bottom corner of the van's passenger door open with the bit of wood, just enough to make a gap so I could push the conduit through. I used the conduit to open the lock handle on the inside of the door. The theory is simple but it took me one hour of pure concentration to open the door like this. I got in, put all my shopping away and went to bed. That never happened again. This was before I fitted deadlocks to all my doors, otherwise it would have been a lot more difficult to get back in.

Here are four more ways to get into your van without a key:

1. **Use a 'shim'.** A thin piece of material like a 30cm ruler. You can slide this vertically down past the rubber window seal to manipulate the lock mechanism inside the door. This can be tricky because you can't see the mechanism inside, and most newer vans now have a guard in place to stop people doing this.
2. **Remove window.** If you have a fixed window that sits in a rubber seal (like many camper vans have) you might be able to pull the seal out that holds the glass in place. It's not easy though. You might need some soap on the rubber and a lot of care not to break the glass.
3. **Get a locksmith.** This will cost you a lot but a

locksmith can get into pretty much any car without causing damage.

4. **Have a photo of your key.** A locksmith will be able to make you a new key from a clear photograph. Take a picture of your key and keep it on your phone.

Never lock yourself out again

I now have a spare key hidden underneath the van incase I ever lock myself out or lose the key. This key doesn't have a transponder chip in it (it will open the doors but it can't start the engine) so if someone found it, they wouldn't be able to drive away. These keys are cheaper to get made (about £10) because it's just the mechanical part that needs to be cut without the electronic transponder part, which would cost around £50. To make it a bit more difficult, I covered the key in thick, sticky grease. I also have the other key (for the deadlocks) hidden under the van in a different place, so someone would have to find both keys to get in.

Essential safety equipment

If your van is made of wood, you must be careful of open flames. If you're driving on the road, be careful. If you're cooking chips in five inches of hot oil, don't pop out to the shops. Be careful. But also, you should carry some some essential safety items in your van, some of which could save your life and the van's life.

Fire extinguisher

All the different types of fire extinguisher can be confusing. They seem to change their minds from year to year about what extinguisher should be used on what fire. All I know is that powder is one of the most versatile, and is carried in all caravans and motorhomes – it's just very messy if you have to use it.

I mounted this 1KG extinguisher on the inside of my side

door so it can easily be accessed from the outside and inside. This is only going to work for very small fires, lasting just several seconds before it runs out. I wouldn't get anything smaller than 1KG – pretty much useless when the van is made of wood.

Fire blanket

I keep a fire blanket under the hob. Hot oil in a pan can easily go up in flames and it's probably a bit more dangerous in a van than a house because it's such an enclosed space and a fire wouldn't take long to spread. Put the fire blanket in an obvious place near the cooker and make sure it can be pulled out easily.

Smoke alarm

You've probably got one of these in your house already. You'll just need to buy a battery for it and put it in the van. Although, in a van, you'd probably know about a fire long before a smoke alarm does, compared to in a house. But at least you might be able to hear it when you're at the shops whilst the chips are doing. My smoke alarm is fixed to the ceiling near the front of the van, where I won't knock it off with my head.

Carbon monoxide (CO) alarm

Everyone should have one of these in their van. In my opinion it's more important than a smoke alarm. At least with smoke you can see it. Carbon monoxide has no smell and it cannot be detected by humans. It's odourless, tasteless and colourless.

Remember, a CO alarm does not detect propane or butane gas, or gas leaks. It detects the presence of the highly poisonous carbon monoxide gas, which is produced by incomplete burning of carbon containing materials – basically any fuel – like wood, gas or petrol. If a gas appliance develops a fault, or the chimney of your wood burner is blocked, or there is not enough oxygen in the room, it can cause incomplete combustion and CO gas will be produced. You will not detect it without an alarm.

Quite often with gas appliances, a yellow, sooty, flappy flame can be an indication of a fault, and it's likely that CO gas is being produced. Gas should burn blue, maybe with slight yellow/orange tips but mainly blue.

In my van I have a CO detector with a digital readout so I can always see if the value starts to creep up. No matter what detector you get, it will have an audible alarm which sounds if the CO level becomes too high over a certain period of time. The batteries in these detectors are usually not replaceable, but last up to seven years.

Battery safety

You probably have a separate bank of batteries to power the living space of your van. Most of the time it will be a flooded lead acid type of battery, which can pose a few risks and cause damage if not properly looked after. You'll be able to find information on how to look after your batteries in the data sheet supplied with them. But generally, you should be observant of any of the following signs:

- **Excessive heat.** Batteries should only warm up slightly during charge. If they are getting hot check the charge voltage and the electrolyte level. You can find this information on the manufacturer's data sheet that comes with the batteries.
- **Bulging or split casing.** Replace battery. Do not use.
- **Excessive fizzing or bubbling sound.** The fizzing sound is hydrogen gas. A small amount is normal but it shouldn't be excessive or violently fizzing. This often happens because of overcharging due to a high charge voltage – sometimes caused by a faulty

charger or a short between battery plates.

- **Strange smells.** Sulphur (like an eggy smell) or burning plastic. New batteries can sometimes give off a smell like this but it should disappear after the first few charges. A plastic smell would indicate overheating, causing the plastic casing to heat up, which is not normal.

- **Loss of electrolyte.** Never use or charge a battery that has low electrolyte. Most flooded lead acid batteries have a way to check the electrolyte level. With maintenance-free batteries you'll have a float (usually a small, green coloured ball) and a small transparent window that's viewed from the top of the battery. If you can't see the float when the battery is fully charged, chances are it needs to be replaced. With serviceable batteries you have to remove the caps on the top to check the electrolyte levels. The level should always cover the whole of the lead plates plus a few centimetres extra.

- **Signs of leaks.** No battery should ever leak. By keeping your batteries clean you'll easily be able to spot signs of leaking. Have it checked and replaced if necessary.

Gas safety and checking for leaks

Gas can be dangerous, but it's perfectly safe when used with caution and vigilance. Although this is no excuse for a poor installation, and every effort should be made to make sure it is as safe as possible to start with – getting the system checked by someone, for example.

It's usually fairly obvious if gas leaks – it really does stink. The smell is an intentional 'warning agent' that is added when the gas is processed so we can easily detect a leak with our noses. It works well.

But there's another very simple test you can do yourself to make sure there is not even the slightest leak anywhere in the system:

1. Turn on the main gas supply so gas runs to all appliances – with appliances not running.
2. Now turn the gas supply off. The gas should be trapped in the pipes and should stay there, unless there is a leak.
3. Wait a few hours or even a day.
4. Disconnect a pipe in the system. I disconnected the main pipe from the gas regulator. There should be a small burst of gas that will escape. If no gas comes out, you know it must have escaped through a leak.

Have it checked

You should feel safe in your van. If you don't, you should get it checked out by another person and have any problems or high-risk things sorted out. It doesn't have to be the official health and safety executive, but it should at least be someone who has experience with van conversions, electrics and gas installations. Most motorhome suppliers will be able to do this or recommend someone who can.

11

Travelling happy

In this chapter I'll share some of the things I've learnt from the past few years of full-time
travel in my van, and I'll answer some questions I often get about travelling.

The travel itinerary

If you're really keen on seeing loads of things and places with very limited time then a travel itinerary will help you do that. Although, if you're trying to 'do Europe' in three months, I'd probably suggest chilling. Quality is better than quantity. And if you travel too quickly, you're just driving.

I've never really had a travel plan or itinerary. I don't know exactly where I'm going and I pretty much just make it up as I go along. It would be impossible to have planned these past few years. I could never replicate all those experiences.

I couldn't have planned the time I jumped in a car full of Greeks and ended up at an all night party at a squatted theatre in an anarchist neighbourhood of Athens. And I never planned to spend seven months in Greece, or a summer in the Hungarian countryside building a psychedelic trance festival. And the day I jumped out of a plane, I didn't wake up that morning knowing I was going to do that. Things came up in the moment. I wasn't trying to get anywhere and I didn't have to be anywhere. I was ready to go with whatever came my way. I think that sometimes sticking to a rigid plan can make you miss out.

Every so often I get into this flow. I meet people, they introduce me to more people and it carries on. Amazing things happen. I get taken in all sorts of unexpected directions. Time flies and I totally forget about the concept of travelling and all the things I'm meant to see and do. When you get into a flow like this it's like a roller coaster. The old life can seem like some strange distant dream, like it might have never even existed. Before you know it, months have passed. Life suddenly becomes very difficult to explain to people back home. It's only the people you're with who understand. They know what's going on.

And that's another thing. Being in the right place at the right time is something some people seem to be particularly good at. Maybe you've noticed how some people seem to go through life constantly having all these random, weird and amazing things happen to them. Or the people who always land on their feet no matter what. I find it interesting. It's an art that I've not yet fully perfected. But it is an art, and it can be learnt. And from what I can tell, it's all down to mindset, rather than clever planning.

So I've never had a travel itinerary but I did aways have a vision in my mind of how I wanted things to be. And I knew what I wanted to get out of travelling. I combined that with flexibility, an open mind and a willingness to improvise. It's worked well up to now. But everyone is different. Some people can't help but feel they need to know exactly where they'll be in one day, week, or months time. Whatever your style is, and whether you have a plan or no plan at all, the only thing I'd recommend is to be open and don't be afraid of getting swept away.

Deciding where to go

I've often found myself totally paralysed with options and it can be overwhelming, especially at first, and especially when I'm on my own. Travelling definitely helps you exercise your decision-making muscle – something I've found to be hugely useful in every other aspect of my life. But most of the time, I know I can go anywhere and it'll be good. I will always get something from it. And if a place really isn't working, I can leave and be in a new country by the morning.

My journey was always, and still is, led mostly by curiosity. I'll usually go to the places I know the least about. But there are some things that help me make decisions on where to go:

- **Clues.** I keep an eye (and ear) out for clues and signs that have some kind of meaning to me. Clues can come from anywhere: bus numbers, prices of sandwiches, the time, bits of rubbish on the floor or overhearing a person in a cafe saying 'Berlin'. I adjust my path based on these things. What we see as meaningful signs are usually the things we actually want. So in that way it works.

- **Photos.** Sometimes I look at photos that are pinned on Google maps or on an image search. If it looks nice, I'll go. It's also helpful for finding good photography locations.
- **People.** If someone tells me I should go somewhere, I usually will. Sometimes if I pick up a hitchhiker they'll tell me or show me some good places. Just one hitchhiker might completely change my direction, or the course of my next six months.
- **Maps.** I'm always looking at maps. I like them. If I see something that intrigues me, I'll go there. It could be anything – a big mountain, an island, a big lake, or any odd bit of land that stands out.
- **Google search.** This is useful for finding general information and interesting places, but Google can't tell you everything. The problem is that most of the places at the top of the search results are there to sell you stuff and it can be difficult to get past. But that's why people's personal blogs are useful.
- **Blogs.** A personal blog gives you a good, honest, first-hand insight into a place or country. A blogger isn't trying to sell you tickets or tours or hotels and their opinion is usually (and should be) unbiased.
- **Books.** Travel books are good for general information about a region or culture or to give you a bit of a history lesson. There are many different travel books for every style of traveller. It depends what you're into. I have one travel book in the van: Lonely Planet guide to Europe. That's not a recommendation. Someone just left it here.
- **Feeling.** If I can't decide between two places, I try to listen to my body. If I get a feeling in my upper body (around my chest), whilst saying the option out loud, then it's a positive. If I get a feeling lower down in my stomach it's a negative. So I go with the positive. If they're both positive, I'll flip a coin. It doesn't really matter.

- **You.** This winter I had so many choices of where to go. I put the options in a blog post and people's comments helped me decide. Sardinia it is. Even if you don't have a blog, you probably have something equivalent, whether it's on or offline – a community, Facebook, group or forum you're part of.

For making notes of the places I find (using the methods above), I use Evernote with the tag 'travel'. I might also star a few locations on Google Maps so I can easily find them again later.

16 ways to meet people

On the road you meet every kind of person. And you'll naturally attract and meet your kind of people. I think making friends on the road is so much easier than in normal life. It's like you bypass a lot of the normal BS. So here are 16 ways to meet people whilst travelling:

1. Busking

If you're spending hours a day outside performing in front of loads of people you're certain to meet people. And it's usually people on the same wavelength, who have an interest in whatever you're doing. I met some cool people in Athens whilst busking. You don't even have to busk. Go and make friends with a busker. They might be part of some gypsy/traveller/art/music collective and invite you back to a warehouse where they all live.

2. Workaway.info

This is a great website that connects travellers with locals (hosts) all over the world. The idea is you go and help someone in exchange for accommodation and/or food. It could be anything: farming, helping someone build a house out of straw bales or just helping someone use a computer. There are all sorts of interesting projects listed on the website and it's a good place to find off-grid, eco and alternative kinds of projects. I spent a few months in Greece helping build paths, gardening, wiring solar panels and fixing wind turbines. You'll always meet other people who are also volunteering. I've made some good friends this way.

3. In the street

I've met a lot of people just in the street. When you have the door of the van open in a good city, it's bound to happen. In Berlin, I camped on a street that was lined with vandwellers. We had community. Half of the summer revolved around that street and the people I met.

4. Co-working spaces

These places attract a diverse bunch of people doing interesting things and working remotely from all over the world. Co-working spaces often organise meetups and social events. They are good for networking, getting ideas and inspiration. I spent some time in a few co-working spaces whilst writing this book. I went mountain biking with an author who was working on his 18th book. Woah.

5. Festivals

I spent my first summer helping to build a festival in Hungary. If you're on your own and want to go to a festival, volunteering is a good way to get involved and meet loads of people. I've met loads of festival people who I've seen again, randomly, on the other side of Europe in other festivals.

6. A hobby or sport

You'll be able to find people in your area doing whatever sport or activity you're interested in. And many cities have a daily or weekly jogging route that's open for everyone to join – or morning yoga in the park. With surfing it's easy, you just pull up to the beach next to another van and you're already friends.

7. Hackerspaces

Maybe you're not into sports too much (I'm not really). And maybe you prefer to sit in a basement, hacking electronics and making things. There are many places like this and they're getting more popular. Have a look to see if there's a 'hackerspace' near you: wiki.hackerspaces.org. There are hundreds all over the world. C-base in Berlin is probably the most well known one.

8. Meetup.com

This website is useful for finding interest groups. There's pretty much every kind of interest group on here. You enter your area and what things you're interested in and it tells you what meetups are happening near you. You can even start your own meetup group.

9. Facebook/internet groups

In Barcelona, international travellers meet up on the beach every day. Many big cities have things like this and it usually revolves around a Facebook group.

10. Rainbow gatherings

Hippies, nomads, shamans, travellers, yogis and wanderers from all over the world come to gather on a remote area of land to form a temporary community and live together for a month at a time. These events always revolve around the cycle of the moon, with the full moon being an all night celebration/experience – it's not a festival though. I was introduced to my first rainbow gathering in Hungary. There's no good way to describe it apart from how I imagine the 60s to be. These gatherings spring up regularly all over the world but they can often be hard to find and are usually word of mouth.

11. Raves and parties

From March to September, raves and parties pop up in random spots all over Europe. Trucks, buses and vans all meet up and put on free-parties in hidden locations – it could be a beautiful mountain setting or an old military base. Some of the vehicles will travel in convoy for the whole spring and summer. If you're into this stuff, you know where to look (usually word of mouth), otherwise they are difficult to find and not advertised on the internet or publicly. But you know when you see a soundsystem truck, so ask them.

12. Search the internet and reach out

When I was in Romania I searched the internet for 'urban exploring Bucharest'. I found a photographer whose photos I liked so I messaged him and met him the next day. We explored some rooftops in Bucharest and he gave me some tips to make my photos better. Just replace 'urban exploring' with whatever your interests are, and 'Bucharest' with whatever country you're in.

13. Be active online

After about a year of blogging and posting photos to social media, people started to recognise me in the street. I've met loads of people like this. You never know what can come from just posting photos – whether it's messages from people wanting to meet, or people recognising you whilst you're doing your shopping. Instagram is a good place to start and it has a strong travel community.

14. Other van people

I've met loads of people just because we both live in vans. By living in vans we're able to easily create temporary communities, and they pop up all the time. Vans seem to attract vans.

15. Law of attraction

I'll explain this separately in a second.

16. Look at people

We get so used to keeping ourselves to ourselves. Out and

about we cross paths with so many interesting people and potential friends. At the very most we say 'sorry' or 'excuse me'. Hold the gaze for a bit longer. Be a weirdo. Who cares.

Last week I was sat in the laundrette writing this book. A girl sat next to me offered me a strawberry. I took the smallest one. She said I didn't have to take the smallest one. Then we spent a really nice week together exploring Sicily in the van. I don't know how these things work. Always accept gifts from strangers, whether strawberries or smiles.

The law of attraction

About a year before I quit my job I started getting interested in the law of attraction. I read a load of books about it. I became fascinated. The LOA, if you don't know, says that you attract into your life whatever you think about the most, and that your external world is constantly seeking to align with your internal world – your thoughts and beliefs. So by simply creating and shaping our thoughts we can change and shape our whole life and reality. I was sceptical.

I did some experiments. They all worked. I read more books and did more experiments. They worked. I started to wonder why no one had ever told me about this. I realised that whenever something has worked for me in the past, and whenever I've been successful at something, I've been using the law of attraction without even knowing. We all use it naturally. But by being conscious of it, we can leverage it to a much higher level to create a life way beyond what we thought possible.

I started to become less sceptical. I was convinced, in fact. I even started a blog (thoughtbrick.com) with my sister all about the law of attraction.

My next experiment was what I called 'Project Vandog'. I

visualised, and meditated on, exactly how I wanted my life to be and the people I wanted to meet – the things I talked about at the beginning of this book.

After the first few weeks of travelling in my van, interesting coincidences started to happen. The vision in my mind started to unfold right in front of me. Things happened that felt like they were put there just for me. Life suddenly became mysterious, fun, exciting and magical. It was like a whole new layer (or lack of a layer) that I never even noticed before.

Everything I envisioned, down to the smallest detail, has become the reality that I'm living right now. There have been many times when I just couldn't believe my eyes. I'll stop to look around me and realise that everything I wanted has happened and is happening. I've stepped right into the life I visualised in my head. Sometimes it feels like a film.

I can be truly taken back by the beauty in this world – the mountains, the silence of the desert, the night sky and the bright turquoise water of the Mediterranean. But the thing that has really blown my mind is that life doesn't work like I thought it did.

I've never talked about this stuff on my blog. To some people it sounds insane. To others it's normal life. But the LOA is not some crazy new-age theory. It's been around since human existence. It's embedded in ancient history and religions all around the world. Many people who have done extraordinary things, or are just living life freely on their own terms, understand and live by the LOA. The underlying philosophy of what the LOA teaches has had a profound effect on my life and many people I know. When you meet people who live by these beliefs, you can tell. There's a spark. Something in their eyes. They understand the magic.

I'm saying all of this because I think the law of attraction is best practiced whilst travelling. To me it's a big part of what travelling is about: you are fully exposed to the world, open to the infinite opportunities and possibilities. That's when the LOA seems to work best and things can manifest quicker than ever. Anything you want to happen, can happen. And anyone you want to meet, you can meet.

Read about it. Try it – if you don't already. Visualise, in detail, how you want things to be. Make it a daily practice. Reality will align.

I once said in an interview that I'd either entered a new world or created my own. Her next question was 'Are you using the law of attraction?'

My tips for happy travelling

I'll share some of my tips for travelling. Some of these might work for you and some might not – or you might completely disagree with them. But these 14 things work for me:

1. Laugh at yourself

If you're in a foreign country, you'll probably do stupid stuff. The best thing to do – all you can do – is laugh. Don't worry about it.

2. Meet the people

Local people can take you away from the tourist grid. When you go into a home and meet a family, that's when you really get a feel for a place and you learn much more.

3. To watch the sunrise or sunset every day

I forgot about the sun for years. Watching the sun rise and set in all these different and new places changes the whole day. It anchors me into the present and helps me focus and reflect.

4. Always react kindly

Even if you think the person is being rude, react with nothing but kindness and never take offence. It's likely just a cultural thing, or because tourists are actually annoying.

5. Say yes

It can take a while to get out of the default closed-off 'no state' – well it did for me. Once I was out jogging and a guy randomly stopped me and asked if I wanted to have lunch with him and his friends. My default answer would have always been 'nah'. But why not? So I did. Nowadays, I say yes a lot more. It can lead to good things that you may never be able to foresee.

6. Trust people

Having the attitude of not trusting anyone can limit your experience and leave you closed off. I say, trust everyone but be vigilant and aware and listen to your gut. It's a delicate balance and might take some practice (and each country might be different), but I like to think that most people can be trusted. And if someone can't be trusted, you'll usually be able to tell fairly quickly.

7. Get lost

And get used to getting lost. Do it on purpose even. I often have no idea where I am.

8. Slow down

Take it in. See less places. I don't care about the list of countries I've been to. I want quality.

9. Get comfortable being uncomfortable

The area of uncomfortableness is usually where I learn the most stuff about myself and everything. I know it's good for me so I see every uncomfortable experience as a lesson – or something that will make me better. Every year I want to be able to say 'there's no way I would have done this a year ago'.

10. Be thankful

Thank the people, thank the sun coming up, the water you're drinking, the rain, the cashew nuts you're eating and… everything. After a while things start to change. I'm not sure how this works.

11. Live in the now

It's easy to fall into the trap of constantly looking where to go next. It can take your mind away from the present, which makes it difficult to fully enjoy the moment you're in right now, and you can miss out on the things going on around you. Suddenly you're not travelling; you're time travelling – your mind is constantly in the future. So I try not to think about the next place until I'm actually there. I try to notice the details in every moment to keep my mind where I want it.

12. Do what suits you

Don't feel like you have to do anything, or that you're meant to do anything. For example, just because you're in Paris don't feel like you absolutely must go and see the Eiffel Tower. Do what suits you. This is your experience. If you're totally in the flow having a meaningful experience with some cool people (or without), forget the Eiffel Tower. It'll always be there and you can see it another time. The Eiffel Tower is just an example, I have nothing against Gustave Eiffel.

13. Don't listen to negative people

Don't let other people's negative experience of a country or place affect your experience or stop you going there completely. I think it's important not to listen too much to one person's opinion – especially if it's a bored person moaning on the internet. I always try to see for myself and form my own opinion. Before going to Sardinia, I skimmed through a long message from a guy on a forum who had obviously had a bad time. It was enough to put people off and stop people from going. But I'm here now, in Sardinia, and I have no idea what he was talking about. I'm glad I ignored him.

14. It's not about getting from A to B

Driving isn't like the commute to work anymore. I'm not so interested in finding the most efficient and quickest way to get from one place to another. I'm interested in what happens along the way.

Driving happy

You've probably been driving much longer than I have, and you're probably a much better driver. But I will share what I've learnt driving my van around Europe:

- **Don't leave things on the roof.** I dry my clothes on the roof. I've lost many pants, socks and jeans because I forgot to take them off before driving away.
- **Low gear in the mountains.** When going downhill use the engine to brake and tap the brake pedal here and there when needed. Never coast down big hills. And when going uphill it's always better for the engine to rev high, in a low gear, rather than rev low – it's much less strain.
- **Get used to your van.** With my van I cannot turn corners fast or sharp. There are many quirks that I had to get to know in order to drive it safely. If I drove it like a modern car, I'd no longer be here.
- **Careful of the width.** A van is much wider than a car and it can be easy to forget at first. That's how I scraped my van on the side of a house – those small mountain villages in Europe can have very narrow roads.
- **Turn gas off when driving.** This is a precautionary

measure – if you crash there's less chance of an explosion or fire.

- **Watch your height.** If you're used to driving a car it can be easy to forget that you now have added height. The day I set off I nearly sliced the top off my van as I was about to enter a low bridge. Be careful of other things like overhanging trees, barriers into carparks and toll booths. Put a sticker on the dashboard reminding you of your height.
- **Don't let anyone pressure you.** I never overtake. There's nothing to be gained, and my van is too slow. I never want to piss people off but sometimes it's difficult – most people are in a rush and they'll take huge risks. To me, it's not worth it, especially when my home is in the back.
- **Take it easy.** Audiobooks, podcasts and music are all good to put on whilst driving. Combine this with amazing scenery and you'll see there's no need to rush. It's quality time.
- **Make sure everything in the back is secure.** A pan of food falling on the floor whilst driving is a big distraction. It's difficult to ignore because your first reaction is to look round to see what the damage is. This happened a lot in the beginning. But now I use rope, catches and magnets to keep everything in place.
- **Be seen and heard.** Use your horn and flash your lights on mountain roads and hidden corners.
- **Thank your van.** I thank my van every time it starts. I thank my van every time it gets me somewhere safely. Thank you, van.

Driving a big van can be a bit intimidating at first (well I thought so) but you'll get used to it and you'll quickly see there's nothing to worry about. Driving in Europe is no problem. Most of the roads are big and easy to navigate. And I have a feeling people keep their distance from big old vans, especially if they have foreign number plates.

If you're from the UK and you plan to drive in the rest of Europe, your steering wheel will be on the wrong side – like mine is. I've never felt like this is much of a problem and It's never caused me to feel unsafe. It's just another thing you get used to and you'll quickly forget about it.

Picking up hitchhikers

You'll probably come across hitchhikers at some point. Do you pick them up? Is it safe?

In Europe, most of the people you'll see hitchhiking are travellers and backpackers. I've always picked people up and never had a bad experience. I've met some really cool people and had some good times because I stopped to pick them up.

Just because someone looks unclean, unshaven and scraggy doesn't mean they're dangerous. It probably just means they're into good music and have good stories. But I can only speak from my own experience.

In some countries, like Morocco and Eastern Europe, it's quite normal for local people to hitch a lift down the road or a few miles into the village or back. It's usually old people with shopping. It makes sense – most vehicles on the road have just one person inside so why not share a lift for a couple of miles? It would be nice if we could do that in the UK.

Disclaimer: I'm not responsible for your safety. Like with everything else, you have to use your own judgement and every situation will be different.

I heard this story about a girl who gave a ride to a hitchhiker. A week later she got a call. It was the hitchhiker. He told her to never ever pick up a random stranger again. He explained that his plan was to kill her, bury her body and take the car, but she was so kind to him that he couldn't bring himself to do it. The lesson? Always be nice to hitchhikers, no matter what. And anyway, that didn't happen. It's just an urban legend. I think.

Here are some tips for picking up hitchhikers:

- **Be aware of traffic.** Stopping on a busy road is probably the most dangerous part of picking up a hitchhiker. Try to get completely off the road and put your hazards on.
- **Communication.** Make some communication and good eye contact with the hitchhiker before you let them in. A few seconds is all you need to get a good feel for the person.
- **Don't feel under pressure.** Just because you stopped, doesn't mean you have to let them in. If you get a bad feeling, you can say sorry and drive away. Although I've never had to do this.
- **Luggage.** If possible let them keep their bags with them or at least in their sight. They have to trust you more than you have to trust them. They're putting their life and belongings in the hands of a complete stranger.
- **Make them feel easy and comfortable.** Offer food and drink.
- **Any ride is better than no ride.** Even if you get them just a few miles closer to their destination, they will be thankful.

In Morocco I was driving south. My only plan was to stop somewhere before the sun went down. I picked up a couple of backpackers jumping around and laughing by the side of the road. They were travelling without any kind of map or technology, but they knew all the good places. That's how I discovered Taghazout – a cool little surf town. We ate grilled fish on the beach and sat in an old fishing boat, playing music and watching the sun set. We hung out for the whole weekend. I lost your contact details. Get in touch.

Another time, I drove a guy to hospital. He'd fallen in a fire. I remember looking back and seeing his burnt skin sticking to the sofa in my van. He was seriously intoxicated and had no clue what was going on. I didn't get his contact details.

One more hitchhiking story – useful to know if you're going to Morocco. We were driving in the Anti-Atlas towards the Sahara Desert. I picked a guy up who had broken down by the side of the road. I drove past him at first but I could see him in my mirror jumping up and down in the road and waving his hands. So I stopped and he got in.

He rode with us for 20 minutes and was telling us loads of interesting things about the desert. He was a nice guy and he insisted we go back to his friend's house for tea, where he talked more about the desert. He knew a guy who does 'the best desert tours'. He became more persuasive and pushy as we drank our mint tea. That's when I realised the whole thing was a sales pitch to sell us a desert tour. But we wanted to explore the desert by ourselves. He got pissed off so we left.

A few days later, I was speaking to a friend who was telling me he got a great deal on a desert tour because he helped a guy out who had broken down. You've got to give it to those Moroccans, they are the ultimate salesmen.

So if you are in Morocco and you do want a desert tour, pick up a guy standing next to a car with the bonnet up. He breaks down in the same place every day, on the same road, a bit North of Zagora, just after the kids selling crystals.

15 tips to save money on the road

Here are some things you can do to save money whilst living and travelling in a van. Some of these things are more effective than others, but they will all help get you into the mindset of spending as little as possible.

1. Resist street food

The smell of street food can be a difficult temptation to resist – especially after being lost all day from going on an accidental bike ride. But it can become an expensive habit. I usually try to take some food out with me in my rucksack.

2. Waste nothing

Looking back to my house days, I wasted a lot of food. But now, nothing gets wasted. It's just a matter of habit and doing very small things – saving every left-over, eating the core of your apple, not peeling vegetables, etc.

3. Hang around with the right people

Who you hang around with will greatly affect how much you spend. If you hang around travellers hostels that have those loud, holiday-rep, gap-year types selling 'awesomely wicked bar crawls with free shots', you'll spend a lot of money and it probably won't be worth it. Musicians and artists usually know how to live well for cheap – and anyone who has land or who is living off-grid.

4. Stay away from the tourist areas

They are called tourist traps for a reason. They keep you contained in a little bubble and it makes selling to you easy. It's how shopping centres work. Go off the tourist grid and put your wallet away.

5. You don't have to pay to have fun

I remember when I was a kid, fun didn't cost anything. Be a kid again. I try to climb a tree at least once a month.

6. Make friends with everyone

Seeing everyone as your potential friend will get you far when on the road – including parking attendants. In Romania I got a parking fine. I invited the guy who gave me a ticket into my van for a cup of tea. He picked up my accordion and started playing. I no longer had a parking fine.

7. Get free food

Whether foraging from nature or dumpster diving. I mentioned earlier how to get free food in the chapter, 'Cooking & eating'.

8. Cut your own hair – or don't cut it at all

I cut my own hair for the first year. But then I just left it to grow. Either way it saves money.

9. Fix things yourself – adopt a DIY mindset

Fixing things is bad for the economy. But it's good for the earth and it's good for our wallets. It could be anything from sewing up your jeans (that got ripped up by wild dogs) or fixing your phone.

10. Eat the right foods

Don't be fooled into thinking pasta will properly fill you up for cheap. It doesn't. An hour later you will be hungry again, and with a crash in energy. Have a high protein diet and you will be full for longer. You can also cut down on meat (or totally cut it out). Look for high protein and low price (P2PR – an acronym I just made up now, meaning 'protein to price ratio'). Look for food that's known for having complete proteins – for example, quinoa, buckwheat, rice, beans, and soy.

11. Skip a few meals

Most of us will eat three meals a day even if we're not particularly hungry. But we don't always need to. Skipping the odd meal is actually good for you – there's a lot of solid research on this. It will also save money.

12. Share diesel costs

Having friends to share fuel costs will help a lot. You can also use car sharing sites like blablacar.com, which is useful for saving on fuel costs when driving long distances in one go.

13. Volunteer

This will make your money go much further. The second half of my first year I spent just over £1200 on living, mostly because of volunteering – and doing the other things on this list. Check out wwoof.net and workaway.info.

14. Don't buy unnecessary products

Most cleaning products are gimmicky and a waste of money. Diluted white vinegar, or baking soda, cleans everything – it even gets the stainless steel sink sparkling.

15. Consider using alternative fuels

I mentioned earlier about running your van off alternative fuels like cooking oil. If done right, with the correct engine modifications, it can save you a lot of money – and depending on where you source the oil from it might even be free. But if done wrong it can cause engine damage and cost you money in the long term. So do the proper research if you go down this route.

12

Entertainment & technology

I've had to adapt some of my hobbies when moving into the van. In every house I've lived there has always been some kind of electronics workshop in the corner of my bedroom, and it takes up a lot of space. It's the same for music stuff. But now, I can pretty much do all of what I was doing, on a computer. And if it can't be done on the computer, you can get the software to make the software to do it on a computer.

You might have to give up some things when you move into a van. But technology is amazing and it lets us live mobile lives with minimal compromise. For example, you might not be able to bring all of your 12" records but you can certainly bring all your music, and books and films – and they can all fit into a box smaller than the size of your hand.

Music

I have my whole music collection with me. The library I've built up since I was 14 years old: cassettes, vinyl, radio recordings, CDs and MP3s are all compiled onto an indexed iTunes library. I'm so glad I'm alive in this age.

For playing music in the van (in the living area and in the cab whilst driving) I use an iPod Classic that holds 160GB of music. In my opinion these are still the best portable music players available. I bought mine secondhand four years ago and it's still going strong. If you need to hold more music you can upgrade the hard drive inside up to 1TB – that's a lifetime of music in a fully self-contained device.

Soundsystem

It can be difficult to get good sound in such a small space like a van. If the speakers are too big then the whole van resonates and doesn't sound so good. If the speakers are too small you don't usually get enough bass. But I found some small budget speakers (Behringer C1) that are a good balance between sound quality, cost and size. To power them I use a separate 12V car audio amplifier.

Making music

I recently spent three weeks freecamping on a beach and playing music every day with some people I met. Their van is full of handmade African instruments. Locals would walk past our camp and join in, some staying for a day or two. Music brings everyone together.

When I was in Hungary, I met my now good friend, Finn,

who bought me a 45-bass accordion. I love it. It's difficult to break, it's easily stored, and can be very loud without needing electricity. Now I'm the gypsy I've always wanted to be. This is a nice van instrument. Here are some other portable, van-friendly instruments:

- Jews harp
- Small djembe
- Harmonica
- Flute
- Ukulele or guitarlele (a guitar a bit bigger than a ukulele)
- Guitar – some 3/4 size acoustics can still sound good
- Teenage Engineering Pocket operators – low cost PCB synths for instant fun jams powered by batteries
- Teenage Engineering OP-1 – standalone portable synth, sampler and full music production machine
- Or a Novation Circuit – a cheaper alternative to the OP-1

Computer

For me, a computer is an essential part of my life. It is an everything-in-one machine. With a computer and a van, you can live a very free and mobile lifestyle. A computer is:

- **A workshop.** It's my electronics workshop. I can conduct experiments and try out ideas in a simulation.
- **Creative outlet.** Sometimes I make daft music on my own or with friends. I use Ableton Live software with virtual software instruments that are modelled on the real thing – from rare vintage synths to boutique effects, all on my computer.
- **Entertainment.** It's the hub of all my media storage – music, photo and video library.
- **Information portal.** I don't watch the news or read

newspapers, but I do want to keep up to date with the world. I can collate my own news feeds that have only the things that I feel are important.

- **Communication with friends and family.** I just press a button and I can talk face-to-face with my friend on the other side of the world.
- **Education.** The amount of online courses now is incredible, some from top universities around the world, and many you can get for free. After I've learnt the things I want on my computer I can apply it all straight away, on my computer.
- **A way to earn an income.** I've been making money here and there on the internet for over a decade, but now there has never been a better time to do it. I'll talk more about making money soon, in a later chapter.

A computer is a two way device for creation and consumption. In the past week I've made music and listened to music, made videos and watched videos, wrote articles and read articles. I'm using it now to write this book whilst sat on the step of my van. I can talk to people across the world, design my book cover, create blog posts that get shared to thousands worldwide – all from my 13" MacBook.

Data storage

Data storage has never been cheaper. For £70 you can buy a 2TB hard drive (something that takes up 3x2" of space) that lets you store a full catalogue of films and music.

It's a good idea to store important files on a separate hard drive that you store (or hide) somewhere else in the van. If your computer gets stolen you'll still have all of your important things. Or, even better, have a direct copy of your computer's hard drive so you can transfer everything on to a new computer if something goes wrong.

Last week my whole computer completely crashed and the hard drive inside was ruined. Everything vanished, including this book, thousands of my photographs and a lot of the blog files. Luckily, a week before this, I started making backups to an external drive. Storage is so cheap now and backing up is worth every penny. I use Time Machine on my MacBook that does everything for you automatically and keeps a historical log of files and changes. Always back up your computer.

Camera

Photography has changed my life. It's shown me how to enjoy great beauty in details I never even noticed before. It brings me right into the moment and hours can pass without me realising.

Most of the photos on the blog were shot with a Nikon D5100 and standard kit lens. This is what introduced me to the world of big cameras – it has on-screen help menus to tell you what everything does. It's a great camera and you can pick one up for less than £100 secondhand.

Now I use a Nikon D750 with a Tamron 24-70mm f/2.8 lens. It's one of the most lightweight and smallest full frame SLR cameras available (or it was when I bought it) and can take a good beating that travelling demands.

But I think the best camera is one that you are willing to take everywhere with you without worrying about it getting broken and without it being too big or heavy. There's no point having an expensive camera if you don't take it out because you worry it'll get broken. I try to always have my camera out and ready. That's why I don't use a bag or case.

To store and catalog all my photos I use Adobe Lightroom – I also use this for processing photos since I shoot in RAW. Lightroom keeps everything dated, organised and easy to find. I take photos every day so it also helps me remember what I did that day.

Kindle

I agree it's nice to actually hold a book in your hands. I never liked the idea of reading a book on an electronic device and it's why I avoided the Kindle at first. But I had no choice when I moved into my van. I bought one and I'm now converted. It doesn't even feel electronic and it's like reading a book. The one I have has a built in backlight so I can finally read in bed without a head torch. But I still have a bookshelf in the van for certain books I like to pick up and refer to often.

Projector

I had an idea: a mobile cinema operating out of my van. I'd call it 'Homeless Cinema Club'. Or something. I'd park in the outskirts of a city and get everyone off the street (travellers, homeless, drunks and punks) to come and watch a film. We'd have popcorn and everything. I'd project the film onto the big white space on the side of my van. It'd all be free.

This is very possible now that low power LED projectors have come about. I bought one the other day for about £60 on Amazon, but it's not very good.

Vandog's Homeless Cinema Club, coming to a derelict bit of land near you. If anyone wants to do this, let me know.

Bike

This is a triple-win: exercise, transport and fun. There's nothing like pulling up to the edge of a new city in the van, grabbing the bike off the roof and getting completely lost. But I also use it for shopping and other short trips. I have an old racing bike that I picked up in Austria. A cheap bike is probably better for non-serious riding, and has less chance of getting stolen. But a good lock is always needed.

Slackline

The slackline is my favourite van toy. Slacklining is fun, it keeps you strong, focused and gets you out into nature. Pretty much every city park in Europe has people slacklining, so it's also a good way of meeting people. It also doubles up as a tow strap for when the van needs to be pulled out of mud.

Juggling

I've juggled since I was 11 years old but I stopped when I found out life was serious and there's no time for clown stuff. But then I realised life isn't so serious. Now I'm juggling again. I love it. I have one set of clubs with me in the van and some balls. Like a musical instrument and the slackline, there is no limit as to how far you can take this creatively – I will never be good enough. Juggling gives hours of entertainment; it's portable and can earn money busking.

Electronics workshop

I recently built a small electronics workshop in the back of my van. It includes an oscilloscope, function generator, power supply, a bunch of basic components and a couple of different microprocessors, including an Arduino. With these things I'm able to prototype basic things and ideas. It's all mounted on some perforated board above my fold down desk. To have a look you can search the blog for 'van modifications'. OK, you might not be into electronics but you can have whatever workshop you like – or just an area for your hobbies.

Whatever workshop

My friend makes guitars for a living. When he gets his van

he's going to put a basic wood workshop in the back. Then he can pull up at the beach and make his guitars there. Or wherever he likes.

Everything else

And then there's all the rainy day games: cards, board games, drawing, things with paper and glue, lego, shell-in-cup (you just need a bag of pistachios and an empty cup), science experiments and... tidying the van. I'm just thinking of things off the top of my head now.

Here's another game: darts. I don't see why not. You could either have a darts board inside the van or hang it outside on the back door.

The world

I do have pretty much everything inside my van to keep me busy for weeks – months – at a time. But the outside world is also good. When you can have a different back garden every day, it's difficult to be bored. I find myself constantly overwhelmed with inspiration, just from trees!

My days

Since living in a van, I get up way earlier. I've even accidentally become a 'morning person', which I thought was never possible. What's strange is that I never feel tired anymore. I wake up, exercise, meditate, review the day's goals, work on a current project (usually either blog, writing, photography, video or music), read, take photos, listen to music and make music, explore. I like to go on walks, cycle, run, swim.

The days go so quick.

13

Staying connected

I tag my photos on Instagram with #offgrid, but there's one grid I still want to be a part of: the internet. The internet doesn't just make living in a van more of a realistic option but for many of us this lifestyle wouldn't be possible without it.

Every year it gets easier, cheaper and faster to connect to the internet. When Elon Musk gets round to putting those WiFi satellites in orbit, the whole earth will have high speed wireless internet. Eventually the internet will be free for everyone to use. But until then, we've still got some good options.

In this chapter I'll talk about how I stay connected whilst I'm travelling in my van, no matter what country I'm in.

There are two main ways to get the internet: through a WiFi connection (hotspot) or through the mobile phone network. I use mobile data most of the time and WiFi if I need to use a lot of data – like uploading or downloading video.

There's also satellite internet but it's expensive and bulky – you need a big dish on the roof with a decoder box and a subscription to a satellite that covers the area you'll be travelling. But with mobile data being so good now, satellite internet is not necessary, so I won't cover it here.

WiFi

If you want to occasionally keep in touch with friends, connecting to public WiFi hotspots every now and then might be fine for you. Many parks, public places and tourist spots, or even whole cities come with free WiFi access now. During my first few months on the road this is how I got the internet. If you're in a built up area, WiFi is everywhere:

- Cafes
- Hostels or hotels
- Public places like squares, parks, monuments and tourist areas
- Residential areas
- Popular beaches

Sometimes you can just walk around a town and look for an open hotspot, but most of the time you'll need a password. Here are some ways to get a password of a cafe, bar, restaurant or hotel:

- Look at a receipt someone left on a table
- Try using the telephone number as the password – it often is
- Try the name of the place plus the current year or the previous year
- Buy a coffee
- Ask a customer
- Look on the walls for a poster giving the WiFi details
- Ask staff – most places are nice enough to let you use their WiFi for a few minutes, even if you don't buy anything
- There's an app called 'WiFi Map' that shows you all the WiFi spots around you on an annotated map. It also gives you the passwords – sometimes they work and sometimes not

The only downside to public WiFi is that it's not so secure and it can be quite slow because it's shared with many other people. I wouldn't do any online banking or sensitive stuff through a public hotspot. It's easy to capture data and passwords that fly through the air and if you don't know who's on the network you can't, and shouldn't, trust the connection with your personal data.

Also, standard WiFi is not designed to serve a large area so you usually have to walk about until you get a good signal or stand close to the hotspot. But sometimes I want to be able to sit in the van and get the internet without having to move. For that you can use a signal booster and external WiFi aerial.

How to make WiFi go further

You can use an extra antenna that concentrates the power in just one direction (instead of all directions) so the signal is able to travel a lot further. This can dramatically increase the working distance from your device to the hotspot so you don't even have to leave the van.

There are plans on the internet to make these directional antennas out of household items but they're usually not very good and you can buy a proper one fairly cheaply. WiFi antennas come in all sorts of different shapes and sizes and most of them connect to your computer's USB port.

I bought a 'Signalking WiFi booster' off eBay for about £18 which works well. This is a directional 'panel antenna' and a WiFi card (built into one unit) that plugs straight into my laptop's USB. When I first started living in my van I'd park near a McDonalds (because they are everywhere), point my antenna at the building and use their free WiFi from my van.

Most high gain antennas are directional which means you will only see the available network(s) that it is directly pointing to. The more gain they have the more directional they become. This can make them more difficult to use because you need to aim it precisely at the hotspot location – imagine a more concentrated beam rather than dispersed one, like when you focus a torch.

I recently tried out a highly directional 'Yagi antenna' with a huge amount of gain. It was so directional that it became too sensitive to use. If it gets moved just a couple of millimetres, the WiFi signal strength drops dramatically and disconnects. So that's the trade off you get with a higher gain aerial – higher gain doesn't always mean better. An antenna like this one is best suited for fixed installations such as static point-to-point links.

Nowadays I use mainly mobile internet so I don't even have to drive anywhere to be connected. It's more expensive but it's a lot easier, faster and more convenient.

Mobile internet

Mobile internet (especially the 4th generation or '4G') is faster than many home broadband connections and is covering more of the planet every year. It's replacing fixed-line internet like mobile phones replaced fixed-line phones in the 90s. If you don't want to rely on WiFi connections, and you need constant access to the internet, then mobile internet is the way to go.

Mobile internet just means connecting to the internet through the existing mobile phone network that our mobile phones connect to. All you need is a SIM card registered on a mobile network with an active data plan and one of the following devices:

- **USB dongle.** This is a small USB device that you plug into your computer. The SIM card goes straight in here and it connects through the mobile network.
- **MiFi device.** This is basically the same as a dongle (above) except that instead of connecting to your computer via the USB port, it uses a wireless WiFi signal – so any WiFi device can connect to it. If you want a permanent WiFi connection in and around your van, you can do that with a MiFi device. It also allows multiple devices to be connected at the same time, much like an internet router in a house. You just plug it into a power source (some may also have a built-in rechargeable battery) and everyone can connect to it if they have the password.
- **Smartphone or tablet.** Your smartphone can also function the same way as the MiFi device. You can set your phone or tablet up as a personal hotspot (also called 'tethering') and connect to it with your computer's WiFi connection. Or you can just use the internet directly on the phone or tablet itself.

Most of the time I use a smartphone with a local data SIM card installed. This way I always have internet on my phone when I'm out and about. And if I want to use the internet on my computer, I activate the 'personal hotspot'.

Buying a SIM card

You could use the SIM card that you use in your home country but it will be very expensive to use abroad. So if you plan to leave your home country, the best thing would be to get a local SIM card (on a prepaid plan) in each country you visit. That's what I do.

It's a good idea to research first which provider is best for you. There's a useful website that has loads of information about prepaid SIM cards all around the world. This website gives you advice on where to buy the SIM card, how to top it up, data rates and prices for many countries: prepaid-data-sim-card.wikia.com/wiki/Prepaid_SIM_with_data.

Before I buy a local SIM card, I refer to that website. And I'll consider some of the following things:

- **Data only (for phone or dongle).** Some SIMs are for data use only, meaning they will only work in MiFi devices and dongles. If you want it to work in your phone as well, make sure the person in the shop knows you want to do this.
- **Coverage.** Does it cover the areas you'll be travelling with at least 3G speed? All providers give a coverage map on their website.
- **Price.** Providers usually sell packs of data that have to be used within a certain time (3 days, 7 days, 30 days, etc.). You can usually buy anything from 100mb to 30GB in one go, but the cost can vary a lot from country to country. The cheapest and fastest internet I found was in Romania (10GB for 30 days for under €10 – and it's 4G).

- **Multilingual.** It helps if the provider is able to give customer support in different languages in case you have problems, but it's not essential.
- **Tethering enabled.** If you want to tether your computer to your smartphone (personal hotspot) you'll have to make sure the network provider allows it, because some don't. I usually ask in the shop when I buy the SIM to double check.
- **VOIP enabled.** Some providers don't let you use their data for Skype calls, presumably so you have to buy minutes in addition to data. If you want to use Skype (or any other VOIP service) you'll need to check the provider allows it. By the way, VOIP just means Voice Over Internet Protocol, which means any service on the internet where voice data is transferred.

Coverage

Coverage and internet speed varies from country to country but it's improving all the time. I've noticed a huge difference just over the past two years. Most places in Europe you'll be able to get at least 3G connection (easily fast enough for general internet use), but occasionally it will drop down to 2G in very remote spots, at which point it becomes very slow and hardly useable.

Topping up your mobile data plan

Every operator has a different way of topping up and it depends on the kind of plan/tariff you have. With some providers (especially if it's in a different language) it can be confusing to understand all the different top up options and plans. I've found that most of the time it's cheaper and easier to buy a whole new SIM card when you run out of data. Also, when you buy a new SIM card they often come with special offers and promotions giving you extra data for free, so it's also cheaper.

Changing SIM cards often means my number also changes often. But now I use Skype so it's not a problem.

Skype

I never bother with a normal phone any more. For talking to family and friends I use Skype. It's better and cheaper than a phone and you can even see each other as you're talking, if you like.

No matter where you are in the world, a Skype to Skype call is always free. But if I want to call a landline phone, I top up my Skype account with credit – you can check the rates on the Skype website. I only use this when I really need to, like for example, if I need to call my bank or any other service that can only be dealt with over the phone. Sometimes if I'm calling a premium rate number I'll ask if they can call me back to my Skype account – many places are able to do this, you just have to ask.

Set up a Skype number

Skype also lets you set up a number that has a local area code. The number I have is a local Sheffield (UK) number but it goes directly to my Skype account. If I call someone from my Skype account, that number will show up as the caller ID. To the other person it looks like I'm a normal person who lives in a normal house with a normal phone. It's also useful when you sign up to a service that requires a phone number. So if you are changing SIM cards a lot this is a good solution – no matter what SIM card provider I have and no matter what country I'm in, I still have the same number.

14

Making money on the road

Money is the biggest stumbling block for most people, and it was for me. I didn't know how I was going to make this work in the long run and I didn't have any of the answers to the questions I was being asked: 'But what happens when you run out of money?'. I hated that question.

I was always taught that I needed to work hard for my freedom. Freedom is bought. But how much does it cost? How long does it take? No one knows the answer. It's a target that's always just a bit out of reach. It never seems to end.

I believe in working hard but there are different ways of doing it. Over the past few years I've experimented with several ways to make money and I've learnt a lot. I believe you can create your lifestyle first and then find a way to sustain it. Well, I know you can, because I've done it. And I've met many people who have done the same. Now I know what's possible and I'm convinced you can travel for as long as you want.

So if you're not sure how you might make money whilst travelling, I hope this chapter sets you off in the right direction. I'll introduce you to some of the types of work you can do in order to sustain a mobile life of travel – some of which you might not have known about. I'll also share some of the ways I've made money. And to help you take things further I've included some resources and useful books that have helped me, and that I'd recommend to anyone who wants to make a living remotely.

A lot of this stuff requires us to think in a different way about money and work, because what was not possible ten years ago is totally possible now. So I'll talk a bit about that first.

Forget what school said

Everything in our formal education is part of a funnel that takes us into a job to prepare us for the world of work. It's what life is all about until you leave school, and even after that. But we're only taught one way to make money: get a job.

The education system is not designed to empower people and it's definitely not designed to help us live free and happy lives. So if we want to live an extraordinary life doing the things we really want, of course there will be some gaps in our knowledge. But that's OK. There are loads of resources that can teach us these important things – I'll mention some in this chapter.

Also, the world has changed so much in the past decade, let alone two or three, and the model of the world we've been taught to function and work in is simply out of date. There are now many new tools – and entirely new industries – that give us new options for working and living. So to live the lives we want, and to live a life of freedom, we need to be able to look beyond the conventional options.

The individual revolution

The individual has more power and opportunity than ever before. It's all thanks to the internet. If you have something to share (your work, an idea, your views), you can share it instantly with people all around the world and gain a following and even earn a living.

One person is able to create a product, market it and sell it themselves, without needing to be a big organisation with loads of money behind it. Authors are able to create books and sell them directly to their audience without spending years trying to find a publisher who won't turn them down – and even non-authors, like me, can have a go. Artists and musicians are able to make money from their work – and make a whole career – without an agent or a label. The best thing is, most of the tools and resources to do these things are available for free.

These are just a few examples but it's happening everywhere. The middleman is being cut out. Creators can now go directly to their audience. All you need is a computer and the internet. And it doesn't matter where in the world you are.

We can now make money from pretty much anything. We no

longer have to squeeze ourselves into one single job title and be that for the rest of our lives. We can create our own work and our own job title, tailored just for us. We can be many things and we can use our whole range of interests and talents to create multiple streams of income.

Making money in the (old) conventional world is very difficult. Apart from the fact that many traditional jobs are disappearing (because of robots and automation), there's a lot of competition. Everyone is doing the same thing and looking in the same places. But what if you can make money in your world?

No one can compete with your world, your style, your weirdness, humour and personality – especially robots. The thing that we have is our own perspective so we should use it to our advantage in everything we do. Everyone is strange and unique in their own way. The moment we start leveraging this instead of trying to fit into a mould or one single job title, that's when we gain an edge that no one else can compete with. That's when we become truly valuable, and it's when we can have the most fun and get the most fulfilment in how we work and live.

Well that's what I think. I might be wrong. I'm still working things out, and I always will be, because nothing stays the same.

The rise of the digital nomad

A while ago I got asked in an interview if I was a 'digital nomad'. I didn't know what it was so I Googled it. I found loads of people doing the same thing as me – living with no fixed location whilst working from just a laptop and an internet connection. I even found a link to one of my blog posts. I never set out to be a digital nomad but I did always want to be able to earn money with my laptop so I could work from anywhere. I just didn't know it had a name.

This is the new option. It's the option no one told us about at school, because it didn't exist. And even if it did exist we still wouldn't be told about it because the teachers wouldn't be teaching.

Many creative professionals, in all sorts of different industries, are scattered around the globe working from anywhere they please – in beautiful paradise locations – with just a computer and an internet connection. The aim is to live a lightweight life and not be tied to a fixed location, ultimately combining travel and work. Working like this gives you many new ideas and endless inspiration. We know how much our environment has an effect on our quality of work, creativity and productivity. This new way of working is influencing entire brands, companies and products.

If you want to know more about being a digital nomad and what it means. There's a good community on Reddit: reddit.com/r/digitalnomad.

This is what excites me: being able to make money from anywhere with just a laptop that I can sling into my rucksack and take everywhere with me. The different types of work you can do online, and the amount of work, is pretty much endless. I'll go through some of them now.

Five types of work you can do on the road

The way in which most of us know how to make money covers only a very narrow section of the opportunity out there. So here are some other options. I'll start with the most conventional, which is simply to exchange your time for money.

1. Selling your services and time (on and offline)

This is the kind of work that most people are familiar with. You have something to offer, like a skill, knowledge or plain old physical labour, and you get paid for your time, usually by the hour. An example of this kind of work (without internet) whilst travelling would be things like:

- Bar work
- Seasonal work
- Working on farms
- Hostel work
- Tour guides and tourist jobs
- Teaching English as a foreign language

When we think about working whilst travelling these are probably the kind of jobs that spring to mind. They're fairly easy and temporary jobs – maybe not so exciting to do for a long period of time. But for doing the job of sustaining travel, they work.

You can also sell your services online. Quite often people are able to take their existing skills and use them to make money online, from anywhere. For example:

- **Teaching over Skype.** It could be anything: guitar, a language or coaching.
- **Consulting.** If you are an expert in a subject, process or business you could consult on a freelance basis. And if you know a very niche or obscure topic in depth you can charge a lot of money.
- **Remote (digital) assistant.** There's a lot you can do remotely to help someone run their operations, from secretary work to helping run a website.
- **Anything you can do on a computer.** There are always companies, businesses and individuals who need jobs doing, and if you do good work they will come back to you every time. For example, graphic design work, writing or web development – those

are the very obvious ones but it's pretty much endless.

A popular website to sell your services as a freelancer is upwork.com. Thousands of jobs get posted every day by companies and businesses. If you see a job you'd like to do, you submit a proposal and wait for their reply. Obviously there are many other freelancers on here so competition can be high, especially if you're just starting and don't have much feedback. So if you want to get consistent freelance work it can take some time to build up your credibility and reputation, but for many people it's well worth the effort.

2. Creating and selling physical products (on and offline)

It could be something you produce yourself or it could be something you are reselling. These things could be sold on or offline, or a mixture of both. The only down side with this kind of business is that it requires space to make the products and to store them. Some examples of physical products that some people sell whilst on the road:

- Art
- Food
- Clothes
- Crafts
- Jewellery

I've met people who do the festival circuit in the summer selling their products on stalls, which gives them enough money to last the winter. I met one woman living in her truck who makes money doing tattoos and selling homemade food.

But you can sell things online as well as offline. The great thing about this is that it's always selling for you 24 hours a day. You don't have to stand at a stall all day, giving you time to create more good things. Sites like Etsy and eBay are the most well known sites for selling your products – Etsy is more for handmade items and crafts. These websites have done a lot of the hard work for you. They have cornered the market and they make sure your product gets in front of people's eyes, all over the world.

For the past year my mum and sister have been running a business on Etsy, selling art prints related to yoga and meditation. They get orders from people all around the world. The nice thing is, once the art has been created it can be sold multiple times and it doesn't expire or run out. Everything is stored on the computer and when an order comes they just print it and post. They've also just started selling digital versions of their art so there's no need to physically post anything – this falls into the next category, which I'll talk about in a second.

Drop shipping could also fall into this category of selling physical items online. This is where you sell a product (often through the internet) but you don't hold or own any of the stock. When something is ordered it's sent straight from the manufacturer, or wholesaler, to the customer. The product never goes through your hands. All you do is facilitate the order between the customer and the manufacturer. Your job is to market, sell and provide some customer service. This has the same benefits that selling digital products has: you don't have to hold anything in stock and the order fulfilment is pretty much automated.

I met a guy who travels the world whilst running his drop shipping business. It's all online and he sells mainly through his website and Amazon. The work he does is marketing and selling – something that can be done from anywhere with a computer and internet. He has a very specific niche and he's passionate about what he sells, which is probably why it works so well. He didn't study business and he doesn't have any related qualifications. But it doesn't matter. He taught himself and he's done this for the past several years. Now he's qualified.

3. Creating and selling digital products (online only)

The digital products market is a billion dollar industry and there's no sign of it slowing down any time soon. A digital product is anything that can be sent and delivered through the internet. It could be any kind of file like a PDF, MP3, video or a digital art print like I mentioned above. Some of the most popular digital products sold are:

- Ebooks
- Music
- Photography
- Digital graphics
- Online courses
- Software plugins or presets

What's great about selling digital products is that there is nothing physical to stock or ship. Payment and delivery is all automatic so once the work is done, you can watch the money come in whilst you work on something else. Do this a few times and you'll have a passive income that could cover your living expenses.

4. Advertising (on and offline)

Conventional examples of making money through offline advertising could be things like:

- Creating flyers for local businesses and distributing them
- Selling advertising space on your van
- Organise events or presentations, with a company (or several companies) as your sponsor

But you can reach a far wider audience online. If you have any kind of online following you can sell advertising space.

This could be in the form of:

- **Sponsored blog posts.** A company will pay you to write about their product or link to their website.
- **Sell advertising space (on your blog or website).** Most of the time you'll be paid every time someone clicks on the advert, but some advertisers may pay per view.
- **YouTube.** It's never been easier to monetise your YouTube videos, just tick a box saying 'monetise'.
- **Collaborate with brands.** This could be in the form of a giveaway or competition that you run through your blog or social media channels.

5. Affiliate selling (mostly online)

This category is a bit of a mix between the last three categories. You sell other company's products, earning a commission on each sale through their affiliate programme. But the product doesn't have to go through your hands. You can earn commissions just from giving recommendations online.

I'll give you a quick example of how the Amazon affiliate programme works – it's very similar to most other online affiliate programmes. First, you sign up to get an Amazon Associates account. When logged into your account you find a product to recommend and copy the URL link that contains your unique ID. You share this link (it could be through a blog, social media or even email) and when someone makes a purchase via that link (within a certain time frame – it's 24 hours with Amazon but some programmes give 30 days or even more) it gets recorded in your account and you earn a commission. With Amazon you get about 5% of the sale price. You'll get paid monthly, as long as it's over the threshold (currently £25 with Amazon UK), and the more sales you make the higher your commission. If you don't reach the threshold for that month it carries over to the next month.

Sales affiliates are the hidden backbone of many businesses. Over half of the sales on Amazon are from its affiliates. From the perspective of the business, it's a highly effective marketing strategy – having thousands of different marketing channels (the affiliates) rather than just one. If you look in the footer of many websites related to a business or product you'll often see a link saying 'affiliates' – this is where you can sign up and start earning.

Conclusion

Those are all just some basic examples of different types of work but hopefully it demonstrates that there is more to making money than just getting a job. There are many ways of making a living.

When I talk about this new way of working, and the new options, I'm mainly talking about anything that can be done online. For me, the most exciting way of earning money is creating and selling digital products (category three). This is not something that gives immediate results, and is usually something you have to work at in the long term, but if the result is passive income from a product that stays relevant and valuable over time, it could be worth it.

For more short term, like if you want money right now, traditional options like number one (and maybe a bit of number two) are probably best. But you don't have to choose just one thing, and I don't recommend you do. Experimenting with all these different ways of making money would be a good thing to do to test out what works for you.

How I've made money on the road

Most things I've done to try and earn money haven't worked.

But one or two things did work, and some other things worked a little bit. When I noticed what worked, I did more of it. I think that's the trick: do less of what doesn't work and more of what does, over a long period of time. But I'm not an expert at any of this stuff, I've just learnt the things I needed to learn as I've gone along.

Here are some of the ways I've made money whilst travelling:

- **Busking.** I juggled fire on the streets of Athens for a couple of months. People gave money and it was enough for food but it wasn't much – and paraffin was expensive.
- **Google Adsense.** You sign up to the Adsense programme, put some code on your blog and Google chooses the best adverts to display to your audience. I did that for a while and it earned me some good money. But I took them all off. It makes the blog look cheap and takes away visitors. I've put a lot of work into making my blog look nice and adverts can ruin it. I'd rather not shove adverts in people's faces, because I don't like adverts myself. So this is a last resort for me.
- **Amazon Associates.** Like the affiliate selling I mentioned earlier. You get 5% commission on products you recommend. It's not much but can add up over time. I only ever choose products that I have actually used myself and genuinely recommend – like many of the products I used to convert my van.
- **eBay Partner Network.** This is eBay's affiliate programme. I had a bit of success with it but not much.
- **YouTube videos.** This has been a consistent earner for me over the past five years or so. I had a couple of popular videos that I monetised with adverts. I've also partnered up with various ad agencies and

licensing companies on one of my videos that went viral, which earned (and continues to earn) me a consistent trickle of money.

- **Selling photographs.** There are many stock image sites you can upload your images and photos to for selling. I use Alamy. They take a 30% cut of what you sell, which isn't bad at all. I've also sold images directly to customers who have contacted me through my blog. I recently sold a couple of my photographs directly to a large publisher in the education sector, for the rights to print my images in their books. The great thing is, you can sell photos again and again, as long as you haven't agreed to exclusivity.
- **Paid by the press.** In the early days of the blog I signed a contract with a press agency. They took a 50% cut of any photos and stories sold. I learnt what they did and realised I could do it all myself (it wasn't much), so that's what I did.
- **Writing.** Companies regularly contact me for paid writing jobs. It's usually just a few hundred words or sometimes a few sentences. But it's not so cost effective for me – writing takes me ages. I'd rather spend time creating my own content, like this book.
- **Ebooks.** This has been my main source of income recently. And I find it the most fun and rewarding thing to do. The response from my first book was better than I ever imagined, so I'll do more of that.

If you gain a following online (it could be from a blog, social media, or YouTube) you get contacted by companies. They want a slice of your audience. And they want to show their audience that they have some association with you and the buzz that you've created. They will pay you money to mention their products, write about them or link to their websites. They will even send you their products for free. Companies have big budgets for this. Often these companies are selling a product that's vaguely to do with the subject of your following, but not always. Last month a global tobacco company contacted me for sponsorship.

I said no to all of them. I'd rather create my own content (like this book and other things) – content that my audience actually wants and that has more value than a link to some company's product. So that's what I focus on. It's way more fun.

My blog – behind the scenes

The first book I read about blogging said in the first paragraph that 95% of blogs fail. I agree. I've started about 18 websites in the past ten years and only two (maybe three) have succeeded – by 'succeeded' I just mean people would actually look at them. It's hard work. Most of the time you don't see any results for a year at the very least – and by results I just mean visitors, not money. Blogs make pretty much no money on their own.

Running a blog is not always easy but I love it. It lets me use many of my interests and it challenges me in so many different ways.

One time I cycled for miles down dark country roads to find an internet connection because my blog had crashed and the next morning I was going to be featured in The Guardian. All you could see when you visited my blog was a blank white screen saying 'internal server error'. At this point I'd been working hard on the blog for the past year but it had hardly any visitors. If you've ever done a blog you'll know how difficult it is to constantly put effort in over a long period of time with no results.

But this was my chance. The Guardian. It would be shared online all around the world. I sat outside on the step of an internet cafe with my laptop for six hours trying to fix it. Right into the early hours of the morning. It was the middle of winter and I was wrapped in a blanket. I was trying to figure out all this SQL database and PHP code stuff.

I got offered money and food whilst sat on that step. I couldn't explain (in Greek) that I was just using the WiFi from the cafe because I'm trying to fix a corrupt database because I'm going to be featured in The Guardian in just a few hours. So I just let them think I was a homeless guy with a MacBook and accepted the remains of a spinach pastry.

I fixed the blog. And then the sun came up.

The Guardian article came out two hours later and the whole server crashed again because it couldn't deal with the traffic. I got a permanent ban from my web server. I repeated all of the above for the next five days, and several more times after that over the next year.

It was on the step of the cafe where I learnt most of the things I know about Apache servers, PHP, SQL, Wordpress errors, CSS and XML. I had to. I was on my own with all of this and I needed it to work. I knew that if I didn't fix it, no one would. I couldn't blame the IT department. It was all down to me. It's both an exciting and scary thought.

I can't remember what the point of this story was but I'll share what I've learnt. I've learnt there's a great level of responsibility that comes with doing something completely on your own. In a good way. It's this responsibility that has shown me I'm able to do things I never thought I could do. It gives you power and energy that's difficult to find when wrapped up in the comfort of convention. But also, we are so lucky that every problem, and every gap in our knowledge, is just a Google search away. Knowledge is no longer the problem.

Oh yeah, that was my main point: if you have something to share, if you believe in something and if you love something, share it. You never know.

Useful books and resources

I like books. They can help you do, or be, anything you want. A book helps you skip all the years of trial and error and gives you direct experience from an expert. There are books on everything. And there are thousands of books that can help you make money. I'll share some that have helped me.

The books I'm about to list cross over a little bit into the self-help genre, and some of them have cheesy titles. But who cares. These books have helped me (and thousands of others) and I refer to them often:

- ***The 4 Hour Work Week* by Timothy Ferris.** A guide to lifestyle design. It's a classic.
- ***Choose Yourself* by James Altucher.** This book confirmed many things I already thought about how the world of work is changing – but often sounded too crazy to talk about. James shows you what these changes mean for normal people and how to survive in this new era of work.
- ***Free Range Human* by Marianne Cantwell.** Full of ideas and examples of what is possible with technology to give us many new options for working. There are exercises throughout the book to help you find what it is you should do and how to make a living doing it.
- ***Grit* by Angela Duckworth.** Important lessons in passion and perseverance.
- ***The Slight Edge* by Jeff Olsen and John David Mann.** About making the small daily choices in order to make things happen – your dream. Important

lessons in here.

- ***The Power of Your Subconscious Mind* by Dr. Joseph Murphy.** The title doesn't sound like it has anything to do with money, and it doesn't. But eventually, it does.

Inspiration and resources

- **Pat Flynn (podcasts).** Pat is a good example of someone who constantly creates huge value online and makes an incredible living doing what he loves. The guests he gets on his podcasts are always inspiring and interesting to listen to.
- **Tim Ferris (podcasts).** Tim can be a bit too clever for me at times but his content has helped me a lot. This podcast is an endless source of inspiration and he gets some great guests on.
- **Warrior forums (online community).** There is a lot of rubbish on here but there's also a lot of expert advice, ideas and lessons for making money on the internet. I've had several people on here help me out when I was stuck.
- **Steve Scott (blogger, author and self-publishing expert).** This guy has mastered the art of self-publishing and he's been doing it ever since it became possible. He shares everything and has some great advice.

Websites for selling your services

- **Upwork.com** – for getting freelance work.
- **Fiverr.com** – people will pay you $5 to do just about anything.
- **Takelessons.com** – earn money teaching online.
- **Clarity.fm** – earn money by letting people pick your brain about whatever your expertise is.

Online affiliate programmes

Here are some popular affiliate programmes you can get started with right away:

- Amazon associates (UK): affiliate-program.amazon.co.uk
- Amazon associates (US): affiliate-program.amazon.com
- eBay Partner Network: partnernetwork.ebay.com
- Affiliate Window: affiliatewindow.com

15

Van maintenance & problems

Just like a house needs maintenance and repairs every now and then, so will your van. That's what I'll cover in this chapter.

Before I talk about mechanics and engine stuff, I should say that I'm not a mechanic (or even a 'car person') and I'm not an expert at any of the things I'm about to talk about. But over the years I've taught myself about engines and I've managed, up to now, without breakdown recovery. So I'll share with you what I've learnt.

The 'do it yourself' mindset

The more you know about your engine, the less you have to rely on other people, the more money you can save and the longer you can stay on the road. But you don't have to be a mechanic or an expert at engines to be able to fix your van. And you don't need someone to give you permission to look under the bonnet. Often when you break down it's something minor that can be diagnosed and fixed yourself with just a little bit of knowledge and confidence.

A few months back I met a guy who had broken down in his van (an old VW camper). He was stood waiting for a recovery truck. I asked if I could look under the bonnet. I wasn't looking for anything in particular and I didn't really know what I was doing. But I noticed a rubber hose that had a split in it – it turned out to be the fuel line. I cut the split bit off the end and reconnected it. The van started and he was back on the road. It took five minutes to fix and it saved money on a recovery truck and a mechanic.

My point is, I'm not a mechanic and I didn't need to be. I didn't know where the hose was coming from or going to. I just knew that it shouldn't have a split in it. If this guy had opened the bonnet himself he would have seen the split pipe and would have been able to fix it himself. A mechanic would be way overqualified (and overpaid) to do this. My other point is, don't assume that the problem is complicated – just one broken rubber hose can stop the whole engine from working.

As I mentioned in the 'Prepare for take off' chapter, YouTube is a good place to learn more about engines. And also doing the things I listed in the section 'Get to know your van' will help you get familiar with your van and learn about your engine.

Van warning signs and things to look out for

Engines rarely break without giving you some kind of prior warning. Watch out for these signs and don't ignore them:

- **Sounds.** You should have a good idea of how your van sounds. If the sound changes it's usually for a reason and it needs to be investigated. For example, my engine suddenly started making a loud tapping noise. It was the fan belt that was about to snap, which could have left me stranded somewhere. So I replaced it before that happened.
- **Smell.** Electrical faults can cause wires and contacts to heat up which can smell of burning plastic or give off a fishy kind of smell. Leaking oil can also smell when it drips onto hot metal surfaces in the engine bay. Hot brakes and a burning clutch have a distinct smell but if you're driving normally they shouldn't give off any smell at all. If anything smells odd, it's for a reason, so pull over.
- **Warning lamps on the dashboard.** Don't ignore these. The temperature gauge is especially important because an overheated engine will cause permanent damage. In Morocco, I noticed my gauge was creeping up into the red. I pulled over straight away and turned the engine off to avoid damage. It's good to make a habit of checking this gauge often.
- **Vibrations and rattling.** One time my van started to vibrate whilst I was driving on the motorway. I nearly ignored it but I pulled over to check. My tyre was about to blow. I put the spare wheel on, drove to a tyre shop and got it replaced. It would have been a lot worse if I had ignored it, and it could have easily caused an accident.

As well as being observant to any of these signs, you should also regularly go through some of the checks I listed in the

'Prepare for take off' chapter.

Common problems with diesel engines

I'll go over some common problems that a diesel engine may develop, and what some of the causes might be. This is by no means an extensive (or complete) troubleshooting guide for engines but hopefully it helps a little bit with finding some of the common faults and knowing what to do next. I'm in no way an expert but this is what I've learnt in these last few years, since owning my van.

Engine not starting

Most of the time this is nothing severe. Some of the commons reasons might be:

- **Bad battery.** If the engine is turning over slower than normal, and the starter motor sounds a bit weak, it's probably just a flat battery. In this case you may need to 'jump start' your van – I'll explain how in a bit.
- **Faulty electrical connection.** Electrical connections can deteriorate over time and cause a high resistance, restricting current to parts of the starter circuit. In this case the van may show similar symptoms to a bad battery (above) or it may not show any sign of life at all – i.e. the starter motor doesn't even turn. Bad ground connections can often be the problem here – where the wire from the negative of the battery is connected to the metal body of the van. You can check the wiring from the battery and clean connections with sandpaper or a wire brush.
- **Leaking fuel lines.** When I got my van it took about 15 seconds of turning the key until the engine started. Air was getting in the fuel line because of a leak. I replaced the flexible hose and it started

instantly. Rubber fuel lines can crack and perish over time and are always worth inspecting.

- **Malfunctioning immobiliser.** The job of the immobiliser is to prevent the engine being started by a thief without the right key. But if the immobiliser goes wrong it can cause starting issues. If this is the case you'll usually get a fault light come up on the dashboard when you turn the key. This is a known problem with my van and the (temporary) fix involves shorting out a relay with one bit of wire.
- **Bad starter motor.** There are two common fault conditions of a malfunctioning starter motor and you can usually make a diagnosis by listening as you attempt to start the engine. You may hear the starter motor spinning freely without turning the engine, in which case the solenoid is probably faulty and will need replacing. The solenoid drives the mechanism (built into the starter motor – although not all starters operate like this) that pushes the motor sprocket forward to engage with the engine's flywheel. In this case you can either replace the solenoid or the whole starter motor. For the other fault condition you might hear a clicking sound as you turn the key. This means the solenoid is working but the motor is not and will need replacing.

Here's an example. Just last week the engine of my van wouldn't start. I could hear the starter motor spinning continuously but the engine was not turning. I looked on YouTube at how a starter motor works and I made the diagnosis of a faulty solenoid. I couldn't find a replacement solenoid (I was on a small island – Sardinia) so I just replaced the whole motor (the solenoid is built in). The van started and everything was good. I made a video about it which you can see here: vandogtraveller.com/starting-problem-video.

Black exhaust smoke

The black stuff is excess carbon due to incomplete combustion – the fuel is not burning properly. This happens when the ratio of air to fuel is not right, either from too much fuel or too little air. Some common reasons for this are:

- **Blocked air filter or air inlet manifold.** The air filter can easily be changed and the air inlet manifold is usually fairly easy to access and clean inside – carbon can build up restricting the airflow.
- **Faulty EGR valve.** The valve mechanism inside can get restricted from operating to its full extent due to an excessive carbon build up. You can easily clean this yourself with a toothbrush and some carburettor cleaner.
- **Worn or faulty fuel injectors.** If one or more fuel injectors are worn, too much fuel gets delivered into the engine, offsetting the correct fuel to air ratio and causing black smoke. They are not so cheap but you'll probably never have to replace them again – not for another few hundred thousand miles anyway.
- **Faulty fuel injection pump.** The fuel pump has to deliver precisely the right amount of fuel to the engine. A fault in the pump can offset the fuel to air ratio, possibly causing a black smoke problem. If this is the case it's likely you'll be experiencing other problems as well – like spluttering and loss of power.
- **Faulty turbocharger.** The turbo is a kind of turbine that forces more air, at high pressure, into the engine to increase power. If this is faulty it can prevent enough air getting through to match the amount of fuel in the cylinders.

Here's an example of when I had this black smoke problem. I started to get very thick black smoke coming out my exhaust whenever I got up to a certain speed. I ruled out worn injectors (purely out of optimism) and checked the easy things first. I inspected the air filter, the air inlet manifold and finally the EGR valve – that was the problem. The EGR valve was clogged up. I removed the two bolts holding it in place and cleaned it out with a toothbrush. That was over two years ago. It's been fine since.

Blue exhaust smoke

A blueish tinge to the exhaust smoke could be a sign that oil is being burnt and you'll probably have to go to a garage to get it fixed. Common causes could be:

- **Worn cylinders.** This can cause oil to creep up into the cylinders and get burnt – hence blue smoke.
- **Worn piston rings.** Same as above.
- **Worn valve stem seals.** These seals can crack and harden with age, letting oil through into the cylinders and causing blue smoke when burnt. Worn valve seals are more likely to be the problem when the blue smoke is intermittent or if it is mostly prominent as the engine is warming up.

But before taking your van to the garage, it's worth first checking the engine oil level. If it's filled up too much, it can cause excess oil to get into the cylinders, causing blue smoke. Also, having the wrong engine oil (too thin) can cause excessive smoke.

White exhaust smoke

A bit of white smoke when you first start the engine, and as the engines warms up, is normal. But excessive and continuous white smoke usually means diesel is going through the engine and reaching the exhaust without being burnt properly and completely. It could be:

- **Low compression.** Diesel needs the right amount of compression to ignite properly inside the engine's cylinders. A low compression could be caused by one or more worn cylinders or piston rings. A garage would be able to do a compression check and advise on the best way to repair it.

- **Faulty fuel injectors.** The injectors need to operate very precisely, providing a uniform high pressure squirt of fuel into the cylinder. If the injector is giving more of a dribble than a spray it can lead to unburnt diesel and therefore white smoke.
- **Water contamination.** Water entering any of the cylinders will cause white smoke. This could be caused by a leaking head gasket or cracked cylinder head. In this case you might notice a loss of coolant over time. To check if the white 'smoke' is in fact water (steam) you can put something cold behind the exhaust (with the engine warmed up) and check for condensation.

Loss of power

There are many possible reasons for this but some of the common ones might be:

- **Faulty air mass sensor.** This is used to measure the mass of air coming into the engine so the fuel to air ratio can be set exactly right by the ECU (engine control unit). But this sensor can fail, feeding the computer the wrong information, or no information. It's a cheap and easy thing to replace.
- **Blocked air filter.** You'll probably also notice an excess of black smoke as described earlier. The air filter is easy and cheap to replace.
- **Other air restriction.** As I also mentioned earlier carbon can build up on the inside of the air inlet manifold. This should be inspected and cleaned, which is a straightforward job.
- **Blocked fuel filter.** Fuel filters don't need replacing as often as air filters but they do become less efficient over time. A poorly operating fuel filter can

ultimately cause a restriction in the fuel delivery to the engine, leading to a loss of power, usually at higher speeds or when under considerable load.

- **Limp mode.** If your van's engine is controlled by an ECU computer (most vans made after year 2000 are) it can put itself into what's called 'limp mode' in order to protect itself against a detected problem that has the potential to cause damage. There are several scenarios in which this mode will be activated – overheating is one of them. A garage will be able to investigate further.
- **Faulty turbocharger.** Since the turbo is responsible for forcing more air into the engine's intake, its failure will cause a loss of power and is worth investigating.
- **Faulty EGR valve.** If the loss of power is intermittent and seemingly random, it could be that the EGR valve is sticking or not operating as quickly as it should, usually due to a build up of carbon deposits as mentioned earlier.

Overheating

The engine coolant must always be flowing around the engine to take away the heat. If the flow of coolant is decreased, the engine temperature will rise and overheat. Some common reasons the coolant flow gets disrupted:

- **Loss of coolant.** Check the coolant level in the reservoir under the bonnet for any signs of loss. Any signifiant leak should be found and repaired before driving any distance. The leak could be external (for example, a coolant hose failure) or it could be internal (for example, a cracked cylinder head or leaking head gasket – the exhaust would give signs of white smoke in this case as described earlier).
- **Faulty water pump.** This is what keeps the coolant moving around the engine and through the radiator.

If this stops working the engine will quickly start to overheat.

- **Restriction in water flow.** Check for any collapsed or kinked water pipes in the coolant system. If a pipe has been taken off and put back in the wrong orientation it can cause it to kink and restrict the flow of coolant.

- **Slipping or snapped belt.** The water pump is driven by the fan belt. If it is slipping, or if it has snapped, the pump will not pump water around the engine and it will overheat. This is the same belt that drives the alternator so you'll know immediately if it has snapped because the battery indictor light on the dashboard will illuminate, as mentioned earlier.

The consequences of an overheated engine can be serious. Always keep an eye on the temperature and pull over as soon as it creeps up above the normal level.

Battery warning light comes on (with engine running)

It's normal for this light to be on whilst the engine is not running (with the keys in the ignition) but it should turn off when the engine is started. The battery warning light is to warn that the voltage across the battery is low, usually because it is not being charged. Some reasons for this are:

- **Faulty alternator.** These can usually be repaired since it's often just the voltage regulator that fails. But if you're desperate to get back on the road it's quicker to replace the whole alternator.

- **Bad electrical connection.** The connection from the alternator to the battery should be checked. A break here will cause the battery to not charge and the battery warning lamp will come on.

- **Faulty battery.** A very low resistance in the battery (possibly due to an internal short circuit) can pull the voltage of the alternator down enough to trigger the battery warning light. Replace the battery.

- **Snapped (or slipping) fan belt.** This belt turns many of the auxiliary engine components, including the alternator. As soon as the alternator stops turning (due to a broken belt) the battery warning light will come on.

If you get the battery warning light whilst driving, you may be able to carry on for several miles (more time in a diesel than a petrol) but eventually the battery will run down and the engine will stop. So if you do get this warning, it's best to pull over into a carpark or safe place as soon as possible.

Squealing sound

This is almost always the fan belt. When this happens, it's best to replace it when you get the chance, rather than waiting until it snaps.

If the fan belt does snap whilst driving you'll probably be able to carry on travelling a few miles before the engine cuts out, but you should still pull over as soon as possible. If you do continue to drive, keep an eye on the temperature gauge because the water pump is driven by this belt and will no longer be running, potentially causing the engine to overheat.

Vibration or wobbling at high speed

Any vibration or wobbles at high speed can be a bit unnerving and is usually less difficult to ignore. Pull over when you can. There are loads of possible things this could be but some of the usual suspects (in my experience) are:

- **Loose wheel bearings.** Depending on the van these can either be adjusted (tightened) or replaced.
- **Faulty tyre.** Uneven wear on a tyre, sometimes due to a faulty tyre belt, can cause a lot of vibration when driving and it's best to replace it.

- **Unbalanced wheel.** A wheel (and tyre) should have its weight uniformly distributed, otherwise it can cause a lot of vibration when driving. Lead weights are used to balance your wheels when you get new tyres fitted. Sometimes these can fall off. Any tyre garage will balance your wheels for you and it takes just a few minutes.
- **Loose wheel nuts.** It might be obvious but it's worth checking to see if all the wheel nuts are properly tightened.
- **Objects stuck between wheels (for dual rear wheel vans).** Rocks can get stuck between the wheels and cause the van to vibrate at speed.

For everything else

Google it, because this list could go on forever.

I should also mention that it could be worth getting your own engine fault code reader if you want to take full charge of repairing and diagnosing your engine yourself. With the right code reader you can get access to the status of the various systems and sensors of your engine to aid in fault finding – known as OBD (on-board diagnostics).

Most vans made after the year 2000 will have some kind of OBD capability and since 2003 it became mandatory for all vehicles sold in the EU to have this functionality – earlier for the US. The fault code reader plugs straight into a connector that is usually hidden somewhere under the van's dashboard or glovebox. Any fault codes are displayed on the LCD display and will need to be interpreted using a website like obd-codes.com. For example, the fault code 'P0093' means a large fuel system leak has been detected.

You can get a basic fault code reader fairly cheap on Amazon or eBay. Just check that you get one that is compatible with your van's model and year.

How to break down

The longer you travel, the higher the probability you'll break down, so here are some tips:

- **Stop somewhere safe if you can.** Away from the main road. If you're on a main road, find a part of the hard shoulder that is away from any bends or blind spots. Put your handbrake on and steer the wheels away from the road.
- **Put your hazard lights on.** If it's dark or foggy put your sidelights on too.
- **Let other drivers know you've broken down.** Put out your warning triangle at least 45m behind the van.
- **Get help.** You can either call for help on your phone or, if you're on a motorway, use an SOS or 'call for help' phone. If you need help from other motorists, you could try waving one down but only if it's safe.
- **Show signs.** Putting your bonnet up can attract people who know about engines (they seem to magically appear) and also breakdown assistance or police.
- **Leave a note.** If you leave the van in an awkward place for any amount of time (for example, if you go to find help) it's a good idea to leave a note on the dashboard, in view of the windscreen, with your number and maybe a little drawing of a spanner to show you've broken down.
- **If you have a flat tyre.** Only change it if it's on the side that is not facing traffic and if it's safe.

Every breakdown will be a different situation. Sometimes working on your van (or just changing a wheel) by the side of the road will be safe and other times it will not. You have to use your own judgement in each case.

How to get spare parts

The first thing to do is find a garage, mechanic or car shop. You can search online (or on Google Maps) for phrases like 'auto parts' plus the name of the town you're in. Cars are everywhere and there's always a garage nearby. A mechanic will know how to get just about any car part, and if they can't get what you need they will be able to point you in the right direction.

If neither of you can speak the same language you can use Google Translate – install the app on your phone. When I was in Sardinia trying to find a new starter motor for my van I had a conversation with an Italian guy in a scrapyard using only Google translate on my phone. It took 20 minutes to explain the exact part I wanted but it worked out fine.

Here are some tips for getting spare parts:

- **Find the OEM number for the part you need using Google.** This number is universally recognised by car part databases around the world. It will save a lot of time if you can find this yourself and give it to the garage or the parts supplier.
- **Find the part on the internet.** If you can't find the OEM number, find the part on eBay or some online shop and show this to a mechanic or garage.
- **Take the old part into the garage to show the mechanic.** They will usually be able to work out exactly what part it is and find a replacement.
- **Consider ordering it online.** If you can't get the part in the country you're in, you might have to order it online. Eurocarparts.com is a huge online supplier of car parts and will ship anywhere in Europe for a fair price. It can take about a week, depending on the size of the part and what country you're in. For this

you'll need a postal address – ask in a local cafe, business or hotel.

How to jump start your van

If your van has been left standing for some time, the starter battery can go flat and there might not be enough power to start the engine. You'll need to jump start it.

Usually you need another car to take the power from, using your jump leads to connect their battery to yours. But since you have a separate battery (your leisure batteries) in the living space of your van, you can use this to start your engine. The leisure batteries shouldn't be used as a permanent source of power for starting the engine but every now and then it's no problem. Here's how to do it:

1. Attach one of the red clips of the jumper lead to the positive of the starter battery – the positive is marked on the battery with a plus sign and will have a red wire going to it.
2. Attach the other end of the red lead to the positive of your leisure battery (or whatever substitute battery you're using – could also be a battery in another car).
3. Attach one of the black clips of the jumper lead to the negative terminal of the leisure battery.
4. Attach the other end of the black lead to an unpainted metal surface on your van that is not near the battery. Making this final connection away from the battery is a precautionary measure – completing the circuit may cause a small spark which could ignite any hydrogen gas hanging around the battery.
5. Start the engine. If you're using the battery of another car, start that engine first, before you start yours.

Examples: breaking down

I'll give you a couple of examples of the times the van has broken down and what I did to get back on the road.

Breaking down in the Czech countryside

The battery warning light came on whilst driving in the Czech Republic. I knew that this meant the battery voltage is low, probably because it's not being charged properly. It's the job of the alternator to charge the battery so I stopped and tested it by checking the voltage with a multimeter. The voltage across the battery should be higher when the engine is on (due to the current generated by the alternator that is used to charge the battery) compared to when the engine is off. But it wasn't. The voltage was the same (about 12.5V) regardless of whether the engine was running or not. After checking the obvious things (the wires and the fan belt) I could be fairly sure that the alternator was faulty.

Now my job was to find a new alternator. I did a Google search for 'LDV Convoy 2003 alternator part number' and wrote it down. I cycled to the nearest car parts shop (again with the help of Google) and gave the guy the part number. I couldn't speak Czech and he couldn't speak English, but it wasn't a problem – all he needed was the part number. He typed it into the computer, showed me the price using a calculator and pointed to the next day on the calendar.

I picked up the alternator the next day and replaced it myself using a YouTube video for guidance. Everything worked and I was back on the road. If you read the blog post I made on this (search for 'breaking down') you'll see how happy I was in the last photo. When something breaks I can't help but think of all the worst possible things it could be. It's such a relief, and it's satisfying knowing that I've saved money by not paying for breakdown recovery, a mechanic and a potentially overpriced part.

Breaking down in the Atlas Mountains

The next time I broke down was in Morocco. I was driving in the Atlas mountains, the van started to lose power and the temperature gauge creeped up to over half. I pulled over immediately and stopped the engine because I knew the fatal consequences of a cooked engine. If I kept driving it could have caused serious (and expensive) damage. The first and most obvious thing to check is the coolant level. There was no coolant at all in the overflow tank.

I filled the coolant tank up with water and started the engine. Bubbles were coming up to the surface in the tank which made me think there was a leak somewhere – air getting pulled into the coolant circuit. I kept the engine running whilst I looked for where the leak was coming from. There was water spraying out of one of the rubber coolant hoses that had been rubbing on a metal edge and cut right through. I temporarily taped the pipe and drove to the nearest village where I found a replacement pipe amongst a pile of hoses that a guy had scattered onto the floor. I was back on the road. The whole thing took 90 minutes.

The lesson in both of these cases is to always be observant of the warning signs. If I ignored the signs of overheating it would have turned into a far worse problem that I definitely wouldn't be able to fix myself.

Leaks (engine and mechanical)

I mentioned earlier in the 'Prepare for take off' chapter that it's quite normal for an engine to have a bit of a leak somewhere. Often it's nothing much to worry about and it could run fine for several years without it being a problem. The important thing is to keep an eye on it. If you're losing a considerable amount of oil, to the point where you have to keep topping it up, it's best to fix it. If you're not sure if it should be fixed, get a second opinion. Just make sure you always drive with all the correct oil, coolant and fluid levels.

Here's an example: The rear differential on my van has always had a very slight leak. But recently it got much worse to the point where I'd have to regularly top it up with oil. If the van runs with no oil in the rear differential it'll overheat, warp, wear out and completely ruin it. I didn't want to have to rely on myself to regularly check and top up the oil level – it's too easy to forget – so that's when I decided to fix it.

Leaks (roof and body)

Leaks just happen on old vans over time. You might wake up in the night with water dripping on your face. It's best to fix them as soon as possible before they get worse or cause damage to things inside the van.

But tracing a leak can sometimes be tricky and you may have to dismantle some of the interior to get to the problem. From experience of leaks in my van, the source of it is never directly above the puddle of water – it can take unpredictable paths, trickling along panels or seals until the puddle is nowhere near the source of the leak.

After washing your van, or when it's raining, is a good time to check for leaks. Some of the usual causes of leaks are:

- **Cracked or aged sealant.** After time sealant starts to shrink and crack. On my van there's sealant around the gutter – where the plastic roof meets the metal sides of the van's body.
- **Worn or perished rubber seals.** Rubber seals around the windscreen and around doors start to perish as they age – it's best to replace these completely.
- **Badly fitting doors.** You can adjust the door if it has become misaligned or buy new seals if they are worn or cracked.

For small gaps and cracks between panels, use a flexible sealant (not silicone) like PU (Polyurethane) adhesive used for coachwork building. There's a popular product called Sikaflex-512, which works very well and can be painted over, but this is essentially just a PU adhesive (sometimes sold as caravan sealant) at double the cost.

Battling rust

My van, like many old vehicles, requires constant effort to keep rust from eating away at the panels and bodywork. Rust gets worse exponentially. It goes faster and faster until all the metal is red dust. Horrible. I hate rust. Most of the time I've spent working on my van has been because of rust.

But I've learnt my lesson. I now check my van often and stop bits of rust at the first sign instead of waiting and treating it all in one go. Here's what I do:

1. Check for rust

The first thing is to visually inspect for rust. On a light coloured van like mine it's easy to spot rust and it stands out a mile. When you've found a rusted area you can tap around with a screwdriver to check the integrity of the metal. I talked about this (checking for rust) in an earlier chapter, 'Get your van'.

2. Remove loose rust

Next is to remove all loose bits of rust manually. I use several different size wire brushes on an electric drill. And for heavily rusted areas I'll use an angle grinder with a wire brush wheel attachment. This is easy to do on the outside bodywork because it's a nice flat surface and easy to access, but underneath the van is a lot more awkward.

3. Rust treatment

There are two main types of rust treatment products. One type is a kind of acid that dissolves the rust – for example, Jenolite. The other type of rust treatment neutralises the rust and forms a thin latex layer over the top, like Aquasteel. Ideally all the rust should be removed before the metal is repainted. I've found Jenolite to be the best product for this.

4. Prime and coat

With the rust treated (either removed or neutralised) the surface needs to be painted. For the body of the van you'll want to use a primer and top coat. For underneath the van I'd use two coats of metal paint and finish with a coat of Waxoyl.

Over the past three years I've experimented with several rust proofing products and the best I've found is Waxoyl. It's a wax based coating. The good thing about Waxoyl is that it forms a flexible skin that never fully hardens and so doesn't crack and peel away like many paints or undercoatings. That's the problem with many undersealing products, they start to lift away from the surface of the metal causing it to rust underneath – and you won't notice it.

On my van I used Waxoyl on the whole of the underside and inside the box sections and the hollow chassis members. It can be applied with a brush or using an air compressor and spray gun. The air compressor and spray gun is better because the Waxoyl turns into a fine mist and is able to get into all the corners and difficult to reach places. I borrowed an air compressor and bought a 'Shutz gun' with flexible extension tube off eBay for £10 to do this. The flexible hose on the end of the nozzle lets you spray round corners and into the internal sections of the body and chassis.

Note: Waxoyl is only meant for the underside and internal surfaces – it's not meant to be used as a nice looking finish for bodywork.

Leisure battery maintenance

Since everything inside the living space of your van relies on the leisure batteries being in good working order, it's important to look after them – and they're not cheap to replace.

Lead acid batteries work well and can last many years, but they have to be used in a specific way. If you treat your leisure batteries like you would a phone or camera battery (running them down completely) they will very quickly get ruined – these are two very different types of battery.

Also, if your batteries are not maintained and cared for properly, they can be dangerous. I mentioned in the 'Van safety' chapter some of the warning signs that could make a lead acid battery unsafe.

Tips for keeping a heathy leisure battery

Here are some tips to keep your battery in good health:

- **Never discharge to less than 50% capacity.** The less depth you discharge your batteries to, the longer their operating life will be. You can get a rough idea of the state of charge by checking the battery voltage (when nothing is being powered). For my batteries (Trojan 105) this ranges from 11.5V to 12.7V, indicating 10% to 100% state of charge respectively. Below 12.1V (around 50% capacity) is when all power should be shut off to prevent discharging any more – many solar charge controllers will have this functionality built in.
- **Don't undercharge the battery.** Undercharging a battery will dramatically decrease its life so make sure you set your charger up using the proper charge voltage for your batteries. This is given on the data

sheet that comes with the battery and is usually given as two different voltages for the two main stages of charging – bulk and float. For my batteries it's 14.8V and 13.5V respectively – I set these numbers on my solar charge controller.

- **Overcharge every now and then.** It's good to give the battery a slight overcharge (called an 'equalise charge') every one to three months to equalise the individual cells in the battery. The recommended equalise charge voltage for my batteries is 16.2V

- **Never leave your batteries discharged.** Always try to recharge the battery as soon as possible. Otherwise lead sulfate can start to form on the battery plates (a process called sulfation) and eventually cause the battery to fail – that's the main cause of failure in a lead acid battery.

Do your leisure batteries need replacing?

Leisure batteries can last anything from one year to ten years. It will vary a lot depending on how well they have been looked after and how they have been used.

But how do you know if your batteries are at the end of their life? The most accurate way to test a leisure battery is to measure the electrolyte (the battery acid) with a hydrometer after a full charge. This is a cheap device (under £5) that measures specific gravity – which increases as a battery is charged. If the needle is in the red after a full charge, the battery is most likely dead.

If your battery does not give you access to the electrolyte (for example, if it is 'maintenance-free' and fully sealed) there are a couple of other signs that can indicate a dead battery. The first sign is if the battery voltage drops significantly (although a small drop is normal) when under load, even though it appears to be fully charged. The battery will slowly get worse and eventually the load will pull the voltage down so much that the battery becomes unusable.

The other sign is that the battery might charge and discharge quickly, indicating reduced capacity. Or it could take a very long time to charge and discharge very quickly.

Choosing new batteries based on cost per cycle

There are loads of different batteries to choose from and it's difficult to know which ones to buy, so here's a tip. The battery manufacturer will give the amount of cycles you can expect to get from their battery. Instead of just looking at the base cost of the battery it's better to calculate the cost per cycle to give you an idea of how much usable life you'll get for your money.

To calculate the cost per cycle you divide the amount of expected cycles (taken from the manufacturer's website) by the price of the battery. When comparing batteries in this way you have to make sure that the expected cycles are quoted for the same depth of discharge for each battery. Recently I changed the batteries in my van. I compared these two flooded lead acid batteries:

- Option 1: Varta LDF230. 200 cycles at 50% discharge depth. Cost for 460Ah (x2 units at 230Ah each) = £360. Cost per cycle = 360/200 = £1.80
- Option 2: Trojan 105 225Ah. 1200 at 50% discharge depth. Cost for 450Ah (x4 units at 225Ah each) = £397 Cost per cycle = 397/1200 = £0.33

The Trojan battery is a clear winner. For an extra £40 you can get something that will last five times longer.

16

Fears, excuses & actually doing it

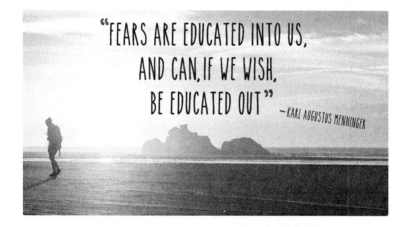

"FEARS ARE EDUCATED INTO US, AND CAN, IF WE WISH, BE EDUCATED OUT" — KARL AUGUSTUS MENNINGER

I get messages every day from people saying they wish they could do what I'm doing BUT... the rest of the sentence is some reason they can't do what I've done. I also had many of these same thoughts. We can call them fears or we can call them excuses, but they're usually the same thing. I'll share some with you, giving my thoughts on each.

'What if the van breaks down?'
It probably will. But vans can be fixed and there's always a

guy who knows a good mechanic in pretty much every town and city throughout the world. If you want a bit more peace of mind, get breakdown cover or learn about your engine, or both.

'I'll be lonely'

To me, lonely is spending eight hours a day working with people who don't really understand me in a job that doesn't stimulate me or let me express my range of interests. Lonely is having to try and fit into a way of living I'm told I must fit into and enjoy in order to be 'normal'.

It might be a bit scary at first leaving your normal 'herd' but you'll meet loads of new people. I think meeting people whilst travelling is a lot easier than in conventional life. And being in a van, you are completely open to the world – compared to the sheltered bubble of an office job. Also, it's now easier than ever to stay in touch with family and friends whilst also making new friends, no matter where you are. See the section about meeting people in the chapter, 'Travelling happy'.

'I don't have any money'

Decide how much you need. Sell what you can and save what you can. It's just a matter of time. When you have enough money for a van, move into it (and out of your house) whilst you continue to earn your normal wage. Once you're on the road, there are plenty of ways to earn money. Read books on making money – see the chapter 'Making money on the road'. Remember, you'll need nothing like the amount of money needed when you're living a conventional life.

'I'll have no routine'

You don't need someone else to give you a routine. When you live in a van you can be your own master. That's when things get interesting. You can even make up your own calendar, with your own days of the week and your own months, if you like.

'I'll end up broke with no money'
This can happen no matter what we do. But at least you'll always have a roof over your head, and you won't get kicked out of your home for not being able to pay rent.

'I'll smell because I won't be able to wash properly'
It's difficult to smell really bad. I've tried. It's quite easy to stay clean and wash properly. See the chapter 'Toilet & washing'.

'It'll look bad on my CV'
You thought for yourself and went off on your own to do something that excited you. You're independent, curious and you have initiative. You didn't follow the herd. I think you'd make a good employee. And at least your CV will be a bit different. But maybe I'm wrong. What do I know? I don't have a CV. Just remember… life.

And if it helps, I feel like the benefits I've gained from doing all of this far outweigh a few 'missing' years on my (hypothetical) CV. I feel like the things I've learnt in these past few years have been more valuable than all my years of education and employment put together. I can't talk for others, but for me, the kind of personal development that is gained from travelling (and from everything I've done in the past few years) has a lot more value than how good I can make myself look on a bit of paper.

'I don't have the skills to convert a van'
No one has the skills at first. Basic DIY skills help but they're not essential. You can learn how to cut wood straight in one afternoon. Take it step by step and break it up into as many small projects as you need – you don't have to learn everything in one go. You can convert a van into your home, and it doesn't really take a huge amount of skill. See the van

conversion section of my blog, and also my first book, *From Van to Home.*

'I'm not sure I can drive something that big'

You'll quickly get used it. A van is tiny compared to some of the other things on the road. Just take it easy at first and it'll quickly become second nature.

'I own a house'

Rent it and let that money pay the mortgage. Any leftover cash every month can go towards travelling. Or just sell the house.

'What if someone breaks into the van?'

We can only do our best to keep the van secure and follow some of the things I talked about in the 'Van safety' chapter. After that, there's no point worrying. If you have good insurance hopefully you'll be able to claim for the damages plus stolen items.

'I know nothing about engines'

It's not absolutely necessary to know about engines. But chances are, you'll pick things up as you go along.

'People will think I'm crazy'

That's alright. Leave them to their lives. You know what you need to do to make you happy. If you want to do something extraordinary you have to do something not ordinary. I'd rather someone call me crazy than not crazy.

'What If I regret this later on?'

I've never met anyone who has regretted travelling. I've never heard anyone say 'I wish I didn't travel' or 'I wish I travelled less when I was younger'.

'I'm too old'

If you weren't too old you'd be too young. It's an excuse. Forget about your age and get on with your life. Go and do it. There's a reader of the blog, Hans, he's 70 (sorry Hans, the secret's out). Hans kite surfs and lives and travels in a van. He's living life. When you talk to him, you would never guess he's 70. The number means nothing. Saying you're 'too old' will make you start to believe it and you'll age way before your time. Then you'll be in a hospital bed thinking 'NOW I'm too old'.

'I don't feel ready'

Can you think of a time when you will be ready? Put that in your calendar. If you miss that date you'll probably never feel ready, in which case, leave tomorrow.

'I have kids'

If you already have kids, how much more difficult can it really get? So take them with you. I don't have kids so it's easy for me to say, but I've met loads of families who travel in a van with kids. You won't know unless you try it. I have never met more amazing kids than ones who travel. They eat good food, spend a lot of time outside, are highly sociable and their curiosity about the world is constantly being fed. Those kids will grow up to be amazing.

'I want to travel but with everything that's happening at the moment in the world I don't know if it's a good idea' (referencing current media and news stories).

Turn the TV off! This is the best time to go. It feels like there is a lot of disruption and unsettlement in the world at the moment. Everything is breaking. Everything is in decline. Blah blah blah. The news has been telling us this for decades. Go and be happy. Happy people is what the world needs. The news is not the world. Ignore.

'I can't quit my job'

We live on a big round rock floating in nothingness. This

particular rock we call Earth, but there are 1,000,000,000,000,000,000,000,000 more floating rocks (actual number), and that's just in our observable universe – and there are more universes. At the moment there is a genuine fear among scientists that the rock we live on will get hit by a big asteroid, wiping out our existence. It's not unlikely either. It'll happen at some point, and probability-wise, we're due.

We're so lucky to have the chance to explore Earth in the time that it is alive, and in the time that we are alive. You can get another job but not another life, and not another Earth. Enjoy it. There's no time to waste.

Note: be careful of being in this perspective for too long. It's a crazy place to be. Zoom back in now. In in in. Plus plus plus.

'What if I turn into a hippy?'
Don't worry. It happens. Things happen.

About the scared bit of the brain

The other day I met with a reader of the blog, Chris. He asked me if I wanted to jump out of a plane with him. I said yeah but I was terrified. The scared bit of my brain was screaming, telling me not to do it. I couldn't make it understand that everything will be fine because I have a guy on my back who has a parachute on his back and we'll safely float down to the ground. This scared part of the brain is not always helpful. It can be difficult to control or reason with.

I wanted to have fun and jump out of a plane but my brain wouldn't let me. Just like I wanted to travel, but my brain kept telling me 'NO. It's dangerous. You can't.'. It's this deep unconscious part of the brain (the scared bit) that's mostly in control, not us. We just have to try and get it to do what we want. It can take a lifetime to master. I'm not there yet.

It would have been easier to say no to Chris and not jump out of a plane at 14000ft – maybe go to the beach, wander around with my camera or read a book instead. But I jumped and it was amazing, and then I went to the beach. Thank you, Chris.

What I'm saying is, this scared bit of the brain doesn't always know what's best for us. It's running old software. It often gets things wrong and sometimes we have to ignore it, or just tip toe around it.

You can do this

I wanted to do this so much – to live in a van and travel, and be (sustainably) free. But it seemed so crazy and impossible and so far out of my reach, especially doing it alone. It would have been much easier not to do any of this, carrying on comfortably in my job and saving up money. But I'm glad I didn't. This whole thing has been totally worth it on so many different levels, and in ways I never expected.

If you're trying to do this on your own, I know how overwhelming it can be. But start by doing just one little thing every day that moves you closer. In the beginning it doesn't matter how small it is. Deal with each challenge in isolation and it will all come together. One thing I think really helped me was keeping a strong image in my head of exactly what I wanted – using the LOA as I mentioned earlier in the chapter, 'Travelling happy'.

You might not need these words of encouragement. I'm writing this because I know it would have helped me a few years ago, and like much of this book, I've written it with my former self in mind.

So here are some more words: you *can* do this, and you can

do it for as long as you want. I wouldn't say that if I didn't fully believe it.

17

About my van

I often get questions about what thing I have, or what the power of that thing is I have. So here's a summary of the equipment, features and functionality of my van.

- **Van:** LDV Convoy LWB high-top with 2.4 Ford Duratorq Diesel injection engine
- **Fuel efficiency (MPG):** average of 25 (28 on flat and less than 20 in mountains and cities)
- **Mileage:** 115000 miles
- **Floor space of van:** 302cm length by 200cm width
- **Roof rack:** galvanised wire tray type. Made by SDV

roof racks, England. 303cm length by 153.5cm width by 13cm depth

- **External dimensions of van:** 279cm height by 554cm length by 237cm width (including wing mirrors)
- **Fresh water tank:** Fiamma 70L. This lasts me about ten days as my only water source for cooking, heating and washing
- **Grey water tank:** custom made 18L with drain valve underneath
- **Kitchen unit:** Dimensions are 120cm width by 42cm depth and 92cm height. The stainless steel cooker and sink unit is from a caravan
- **Bed:** Expands to sleep two people comfortably and the hammock can sleep one. Depth of the bed is 72cm normally (sofa) and 115cm expanded
- **Work area:** fold down desk 75cm width by 38cm depth
- **Toilet:** Thetford C-200CW (manual flush version). This hardly gets used
- **Shower:** Water saving shower head
- **Water heater:** 8L/minute LPG powered instant heater (no tank)
- **Space heater:** Propex Compact 1600
- **Gas cylinder:** Gaslow direct fill bottle 11kg version. This holds about 20L of gas and lasts me for a good few months of cooking every day
- **Solar panels:** 2x100W monocrystalline panels. These have proved to be easily enough during the summer and just enough during winter
- **Solar charge controller:** 30A MPPT generic unit (no make) bought on eBay
- **Sound system:** 100W Behringer monitors and 150W 12V car amplifier
- **Inverter:** pure sine wave 300W (600W peak)
- **Mains battery charger:** CTEK MXS-25 smart charger

- **Batteries:** 4xTrojan T105 – these are 6V batteries wired for 12V as two series pairs in parallel
- **Split charging:** Durite 40A volt sensing relay
- **Lighting:** 2xLED clusters in the ceiling (about 1W each) and one 4W LED cluster in the desk lamp
- **Fridge:** Waeco CDF-18. It runs directly on 12V and consumes 35 watts of power. It can be set to either fridge or freezer mode
- **Water pump:** Shurflo Trailking 7 (30PSI version)
- **Water accumulator:** Fiamma A-20

To see more photos of my completed van conversion go to: vandogtraveller.com/gallery/diy-van-conversion-photos.

18

I think that's about it

I hope you've found this book useful and I hope I've been able to answer some of your questions about living in a van and travelling. If you still have questions, or need some help, send me a message and I'll try my best to reply.

Now, can I ask a small favour?

Please could you help me spread the word about this book? It took me many months to put together and it'll take you just five seconds to share it. You can help me a huge amount by doing any of the following:

- Leave a review on Amazon – you can use the link at the end of the book if you're using a Kindle
- Share on Facebook (or whatever) using the share button on your kindle or e-reader
- Tell people who you think might find this book useful – related internet groups or forums

If you have the printed version of this book and you've finished reading it, leave it somewhere for someone else to pick up – in a library, a phonebox, cafe or on the shelf of your local Waterstones bookshop.

And if I don't see you on the internet, I'll see you on the road, or on the side of a mountain somewhere. Good luck and have fun.

Links mentioned throughout this book

Here's a list of the links I've mentioned in this book, in order of their appearance:

vandogtraveller.com/van-living-products – an organised list of useful products I use and recommend

vandogtraveller.com/van-checklist – A PDF checklist of the things mentioned in the 'Prepare for take off' chapter

vandogtraveller.com/reclassify-camper – information (UK only) for reclassifying your van as a camper

vandogtraveller.com/motorhome-insurance – a list of popular motorhome insurers in the UK

youtube.com/user/Paintball007 – Chrisfix's YouTube channel for mechanics and engine related jobs

adac.de – for European-wide breakdown cover

caxtonfx.com – travel cash card

vandogtraveller.com/europe-poi-gpx – a few points of interest to download

directferry.com and aferry.com – for ferry bookings and price comparison

mylpg.eu/adapters – information on the different LPG adapters for each country

lpgstations.com – database of LPG/Autogas stations worldwide

freecampsites.net – freecamping locations for the US

wikicamps.com.au – freecamping locations for Australia

gpstravelmaps.com – cheap GPS travel maps for every device

reddit.com/r/vandwellers – subreddit for vandwellers

legislation.gov.uk/ukpga/1994/33/contents – Criminal Justice and Public Order Act 1994 (UK) – section 77 applies directly to campers

trashwiki.org – info on dumperdiving, freeganism – basically getting food out of bins

locks4vans.co.uk – extra locks for all van types

evernote.com – a great note application for capturing everything

wiki.hackerspaces.org – a worldwide database of hackerspaces and makerspaces meetup.com – meet people with similar interests

workaway.info – work in exchange for food and/or accommodation

wwoof.net – volunteering on organic farms usually in exchange for food and also to meet other travellers

blablacar.com – share van fuel costs with other people

wifimap.io – a worldwide database of WiFi hotspots and passwords

prepaid-data-sim-card.wikia.com/wiki/ Prepaid_SIM_with_data – useful information on different mobile internet providers

reddit.com/r/digitalnomad – a subreddit for digital nomads

upwork.com – for finding freelance work online

fiverr.com – earn money doing small fixed-price jobs

takelessons.com – teach online and earn money

clarity.fm – earn money by letting people pick your brain about whatever your expertise is

Useful links on my blog

If you don't already know my blog, here's an introduction:

Tours of other people's vans

In this series of posts I take you on a tour of other people's van-homes to show how other people are doing it: vandogtraveller.com/van-tour

I'm always up for doing more 'van tour' posts so let me know if you want to do one of your van. If you want me to do a van tour of your van, check my location on the tracker and location page.

My track and location

Here you can find a map of my track, and all the places I've stayed, from the past few years. I try to keep this up to date as often as I can:
vandogtraveller.com/europe-by-campervan-route

Posts by country

Also, I organised some blog posts by country. Click on the country to view related blog posts – many with photos, general info and camping locations.
vandogtraveller.com/posts-by-country

Popular posts

Highlights of 2016 in a van:
vandogtraveller.com/living-in-a-van-travelling-highlights-2016

Where to go for winter (Europe):
vandogtraveller.com/europe-campervan-winter-locations-and-weather

My DIY van conversion

I documented some of my van conversion in this series of posts: vandogtraveller.com/converting-my-van

Guides and helpful info

Posts that don't directly fit under the category of travel:
http://vandogtraveller.com/guides

Gallery

Photo albums from the past three years travelling in my van:

vandogtraveller.com/gallery

Videos

Sometimes I make videos. Here are some of them:
vandogtraveller.com/video

The Vandog Forum

Here you can talk about van conversions, travelling in a van or whatever you want:
vandogtraveller.com/forum

Subscribe to my blog (free)

Get personal email updates from me twice a month (you can easily unsubscribe any time):
vandogtraveller.com/subscribe

Van inspiration on Instagram

Here are some van related Instagram accounts to keep you inspired and in touch with the community online:

instagram.com/vanlifeexplorers
instagram.com/vanlifeideas
instagram.com/vanlifemovement
instagram.com/vanlifers
instagram.com/van.crush
instagram.com/vansofberlin
instagram.com/projectvanlife
instagram.com/vanlifediaries

Other books by Mike Hudson

From Van to Home – how I made an old rusty van into my cosy off-grid home. Available as an instant download here:
vandogtraveller.com/van-conversion-book

From **Van** to **Home**

HOW I MADE AN OLD RUSTY VAN INTO MY COSY OFF-GRID HOME

VAN DOG TRAVELLER .com

Mike Hudson

CPSIA information can be obtained
at www.ICGtesting.com
Printed in the USA
LVOW13s0757140718
583547LV00023BA/498/P